RECOVERY AND RENEWAL

RECOVERY
AND
RENEWAL

Your essential guide to overcoming dependency and withdrawal from sleeping pills, other 'benzo' tranquillisers and antidepressants

REVISED EDITION

Baylissa Frederick

Jessica Kingsley *Publishers*
London and Philadelphia

This revised edition published in 2014
by Jessica Kingsley Publishers
73 Collier Street
London N1 9BE, UK
and
400 Market Street, Suite 400
Philadelphia, PA 19106, USA

www.jkp.com

First edition published as *Benzo-Wise* by Campanile Publishing, 2010
Second expanded edition published by RRW Publishing as *Recovery and Renewal*, 2012
Copyright © Baylissa Frederick 2010, 2012, 2014

Library of Congress Cataloging in Publication Data
A CIP catalog record for this book is available from the Library of Congress

British Library Cataloguing in Publication Data
A CIP catalogue record for this book is available from the British Library

ISBN 978 1 84905 534 5
eISBN 978 0 85700 964 7

Printed and bound in the United States

To the memory of my loving mother,

Nell Johns-Frederick

Thank you for your indomitable spirit, for teaching me by example how to harness my inner strength and for giving me my first mantra: This, too, shall pass.

ACKNOWLEDGEMENTS

I am grateful to the many people whose support during and after my withdrawal has helped me in innumerable ways. For their kindness and care I thank: Iain and Zoe, Mike and Jill, Marj and Abi, Colleen, Jackie, Arlette and my nieces and nephews, my Uncle Hart, Dad, Lesley P, Irvine, Debbie, Phyllis and Tony, Crimson and Leslie, Jenese and Angie, Derek, Colin and Paula, Tony S, Alli, Elisabeth and Malcolm, Pete, Melissa K, Tina, Melissa T, Madge and Marion.

I am deeply grateful to Professor Heather Ashton for having vetted and approved the book's medical content and for her ongoing support and guidance. Thank you to the Countess of Sandwich and the Montagu family for their unwavering support, which has helped tremendously, and to Barbara Bell, Val Bell, Paul Brett and everyone else who contributes to the *Recovery Road* project.

I also thank everyone within the wider withdrawal community (our withdrawal charities, experts and campaigners), all of whom tirelessly share their valuable time and knowledge. Finally, to our valiant withdrawal survivors and those currently on their way to recovery, I am deeply indebted to you for your trust and sharing, from which I continue to learn so much. This is our book.

CONTENTS

AUTHOR'S NOTE

This book has been written expressly as my personal account of my experience with withdrawal, both as a survivor and through my work supporting thousands of people worldwide. Omissions, if any, are genuinely a result of any cognitive impairment present at the time of writing (specifically the journal logs), and for no other reason.

While I believe that informed choice is important, I am not against the use of medication, and I do sincerely feel that all my doctors were well-intentioned. Under no circumstances has anything here been written with the intention to be malicious, slanderous or vindictive.

Please note that this book deals only with coping and managing symptoms; it does not address wider, equally important issues (such as attachment and loss, relapse prevention, compulsions, legal problems, etc.) which pertain to illicit users of antidepressants and benzodiazepines. The book will benefit all groups but has been written with specific regard to the issues of those who were prescribed these drugs by their doctors. When I write of recovery being the usual outcome, these are the individuals to whom I refer.

My sincere wish is that the guidance and reassurance offered here will encourage you and give you hope.

PREFACE

Coming off sleeping pills, benzodiazepines, Z-drugs (a group of non-benzodiazepine drugs with effects similar to those of benzodiazepines) and antidepressants is challenging and can result in losses, isolation and feelings of being misunderstood and unsupported. The concept of a 'feel good' book that would give an emotional boost during withdrawal came as a result of numerous requests from visitors to our old recovery-support website, started during my own withdrawal.

As I shared more of my experience, I was asked to describe what the symptoms were like for me and how I coped. I soon started receiving emails from others in withdrawal. Relatives and carers also began requesting written information to pass on to those too unwell and cognitively impaired to use a computer.

I have included practical information about withdrawal based on my experience, my counselling training, chemical dependency studies and knowledge acquired through my support work. The main focus, however, is on being emotionally safe and coping well.

Due to brain fog and other withdrawal issues, cognitive function is often impaired and this can cause incoherence as well as poor reading comprehension, concentration and memory. Because of this, I use an informal tone and simple format throughout the book. Any clichés and repetitions, such as 'This, too, shall pass' and 'Withdrawal is temporary', are intentional. I hope this approach will have the desired effect of making this book easy to read.

INTRODUCTION

When I wrote the original *Benzo-Wise* book I had no idea that just as many people discontinuing antidepressants as those coming off benzodiazepines would end up reading it and contacting me. More than 50 per cent of the people I communicate with are coming off either an antidepressant only or an antidepressant taken with a sleeping pill, other benzodiazepine or Z-drug. The symptoms are very similar and so are the challenges and repercussions.

During the almost three years that *Benzo-Wise* was in print, I received many emails from people coming off antidepressants stating that the book has been a 'lifeline' and the recommended coping tools have proved to be very effective. Some asked why I had not included specific information on antidepressants and why there were no success stories from people who had taken antidepressants only. I now offer this updated version in response – to acknowledge and validate readers.

I will never be able to fully articulate how privileged and grateful I feel to be able to use my experience in a positive way. When I wrote the first edition of the book I was unaware of the magnitude of the withdrawal problem. It was written for my then online withdrawal friends with the primary intention of giving hope to those experiencing the most distressing symptoms. For it to be considered of value not just to individuals coming off these drugs but to their relatives, doctors, counsellors and other carers is an unexpected bonus. I am pleased and relieved that it is indeed fulfilling its purpose and has even surpassed expectations.

What I am about to share next is extremely important and needs to be assimilated well, especially if you are reading in preparation for your taper. I had an intense withdrawal; you may not. There are people who have successfully stopped taking antidepressants, sleeping pills, other 'benzo' tranquillisers and Z-drugs with very few or no problems; it is possible that you could too. These success stories are not found on the Internet, because such individuals had no reason to communicate their experiences online.

Instead, on the Internet we have the people who are having the worst experiences and may also have had very little or no information and support. So you must always keep this in mind as you read any withdrawal stories, including mine. If you don't and you anticipate the worst, you will worry unnecessarily and become anxious about something that may never happen. It makes more sense to preserve this emotional energy to keep you anchored while you withdraw.

On the other hand, if you are tapering or are completely off your medication and are already experiencing intense symptoms, you will agree that a problematic withdrawal can be, at the very least, upsetting. Discontinuance after long-term use can result in the most bizarre physical and psychological symptoms: from muscle pain, burning, twitches and gastrointestinal problems to distorted perception, anxiety attacks and sleep difficulty. This can happen to someone with no history of psychological problems, as in my case where I was prescribed the drug for dystonic tics. Finding as many positives as possible while the recovery process takes place can make a big difference to your withdrawal experience.

Try to focus on accounts where people have successfully tapered, rather than the more disturbing stories. If you have the support of family or friends, share pertinent information with them so they can have a better understanding of what withdrawal entails. Using a technique that works well for you will be to your advantage. It can be as simple as a breathing or mindfulness exercise, or repeating a positive statement. Do it as often as you feel is necessary. Stock up on a few books that make you feel encouraged, movies that are light-hearted and music that uplifts you. Try to use as many resources as possible to make your days easier without becoming too preoccupied or obsessive; moderation is key. By the time this is over, you will find that you have become an expert at nurturing yourself.

Although the word 'healing' is used frequently here, withdrawal is not technically an illness; it is a syndrome or cluster of symptoms that occur at the same time and can make one feel unwell. Unless there are pre-existing or concurrent medical conditions, this will be the only reason for your symptoms. When the recovery process is complete, the symptoms will subside.

Provided you are well informed, when you experience a symptom, no matter how bizarre, you will know that it is due to withdrawal and not an isolated medical problem. If in any doubt, seeking medical advice to confirm this will give you peace of mind. The most important thing to remember is that as unpleasant and unsettling as withdrawal can be, it does not last indefinitely. Recovery is the usual outcome.

If you have discussed coming off your medication with your doctor but feel daunted or overwhelmed by negative accounts of the withdrawal experience, please do not let this deter you. More than likely, the reason you want to quit is because the side effects are making you unwell and you feel worse than you felt prior to taking it. It will be worth it. Remember, your experience could end up being less extreme and only mildly unpleasant. If you prepare yourself mentally and get your doctor to supervise your taper, your withdrawal should be manageable.

Never stop taking an antidepressant, sleeping pill or other benzodiazepine abruptly (or what is referred to as 'stopping cold turkey'), as this can cause serious medical problems including seizures; instead, taper slowly and stick to your schedule. Don't be tempted to skip a phase of reduction if the symptoms seem manageable. Be patient; it is better to have what may seem like a long taper than rush the process and end up in protracted withdrawal.

If symptoms appear while you are tapering off the drug, try not to resist them. Accept them as evidence that you are on the way to being drug-free. This is the beginning of your recovery. When withdrawal is over, you will be able to celebrate having a clearer mind and a quality of life that is better than you could ever have imagined. The most satisfying feelings will be the sense of accomplishment, invincibility almost, and the relief you will experience when you begin to have glimpses of recovery. While you wait, be as gentle with yourself as you possibly can.

1   A FADED MEMORY

Life was good. Not only was my life good, it was charmed. I was introduced to the concept of one's thoughts impacting one's life experiences in my early 20s, and had become an expert at what I consider to be the manifestation of unlikely opportunities and many pleasant adventures.

This was confirmed during the summer of 1997. After being commitment phobic for what friends and family felt was a ridiculously long time, I gave in to their subliminal pleas and the incessant ticking of my biological clock. At age thirty-four, I started thinking about meeting my 'kind, loving, attractive husband'. I was finally ready. It was no surprise that a few weeks later, I met Dylan. The following year, on Valentine's Day 1998, he asked me to marry him. I accepted. Of course, it was most probably coincidental, but it is more exciting to think that by being ready and focusing on meeting someone, I attracted Dylan into my life.

There was just one problem, however. Compared with what I experienced during withdrawal it seems insignificant, but it was a source of bother at the time. For most of my life, from around three or four years of age, I have had an involuntary movement disorder, which was later diagnosed as a form of dystonia. It causes my right eye to twitch and tug intermittently and my head to tilt to the left with spasmodic movements. In the earlier days I would also walk with my left hand hooked behind my neck. It was not always problematic and at times was not noticeable.

Despite having it, I was able to enjoy a normal, active, happy childhood. In fact, for all those years it was described merely as a 'tic' or 'tics'.

As I grew older, I became more distracted by the tics and explored every possible complementary treatment in an attempt to relieve them, but to no avail. By the time I'd met Dylan I had consulted chiropractors, physiotherapists, osteopaths, herbalists and different types of massage therapists. These approaches contributed to my wellness but did not have the desired effect.

As Dylan and I planned our wedding, I knew I had to find at least a temporary cure. The tics were mild and episodes occurred around every 30–45 minutes at the time, and so I knew there was a 90 per cent probability that my face would do its little 'dance' in the middle of the exchange of vows. If that happened I would become flustered and embarrassed. I was adamant about not letting the tics ruin the day and this is why I went to see my doctor early one wet morning in the spring of 1998.

My doctor first prescribed an anti-epileptic drug which was much too potent for my mild condition. Within days I returned to let him know it was making me too drowsy to focus. He then prescribed clonazepam (Rivotril/Klonopin), a drug I had no clue was used as a tranquilliser or that there was a high risk of dependency associated with its use. It was a low dose and helped the tics initially, reducing them to a few daily. I was elated. I had found the miracle cure and our wedding day was going to be perfect.

My euphoria was short-lived, however, as the tics soon returned but this time more frequently and intensely. Once I realized the medication was no longer effective, I stopped taking it. A few days later, I had the most frightening, violent, involuntary movements. I quickly took a dose and the fitting stopped. I thought I had developed a form of epilepsy or other serious movement disorder when I had in fact quickly reached tolerance (when more of the drug is needed to be effective) and by quitting 'cold turkey' instead had what was my first withdrawal reaction.

When the dosage was increased, I once again rapidly became tolerant and the tics returned with renewed intensity. For fear of having more seizure-type movements, I continued taking the drug. The wedding dilemma seemed imminent, and 1 week prior to the big event, I shared my concerns with my new doctor. He prescribed a small amount of diazepam to be taken adjunctively with the clonazepam just for the wedding. By the time the nuptial day arrived, I was tic-free but also heavily sedated. Despite my being in a near-catatonic state, Dylan and I enjoyed a charming, country manor ceremony and an unforgettable reception with family and friends.

I did not take diazepam again until my taper. But sadly, my dependency on clonazepam had become well entrenched within a year of my first prescription. I just did not know it at the time. I ended up taking the medication through repeat prescriptions for more than seven years. For most of that time I was in tolerance, gradually having more and more obscure complaints and minor ailments, or what I now appreciate were tolerance withdrawal symptoms.

During the earlier years on the medication life was relatively normal. I worked diligently within the voluntary sector in the areas of domestic violence crisis support and counselling. I also completed three years of clinical psychotherapy and counselling training. But gradually everything became a blur: the fog descended on my brain, and I became easily fatigued, emotionally anaesthetized, spaced out and absent-minded. Despite eating healthily and exercising, my weight gradually ballooned out of control. This baffled me but I still did not identify the drug as being contributory in any way.

I also had regular, dramatic visits to the local hospital emergency room. On one occasion, due to a lapse in concentration, I peered at a tube of super-strong adhesive to see if it was empty and squirted it directly into my eye causing my eyelids to stick shut. My neighbour must have questioned my sanity when I banged on his door jumping up and down, shrieking like a psychotic cheerleader.

'Rhys, help! Are you there? Crazy glue's in my eye. I've glued my eye shut,' I cried. He looked at me in horror as I tried to tug the lids apart. When we arrived at the hospital I was immediately seen in a special 'ocular super glue injury' cubicle. It was reassuring to discover that this was a common mistake. I had more accidents that led to emergency visits that year including one involving beetroot – and all too embarrassing to share!

When my memory began to be affected and the brain fog became too severe, for ethical reasons and in the interest of my clients, I gave up counselling and went to do a less demanding job. I made unsound judgements with dire consequences but still did not, at that time, make the link. Although I had a feeling of foreboding and was generally unwell, I had no idea that this was in any way related to the drug.

In an effort to regain control of my life, I started desperately searching the Internet for answers. I eventually stumbled upon my 'deliverance' in the form of the *Ashton Manual*, also entitled *Benzodiazepines: How They Work and How to Withdraw*. This lifeline is written by Professor C. Heather Ashton, Psychopharmacologist and the UK's leading expert on benzodiazepines; it contains the most invaluable information on benzodiazepines. (Please note that there should be flexibility in withdrawing from these drugs and reduction rates should be dependent on withdrawal responses.) I recall the tears gently rolling down my cheeks as I finally identified the reason for my challenges.

The following morning I practically sprinted to my doctor's office, eagerly showing him my printed copy of the *Ashton Manual*. 'Look, Doctor!' I beamed, 'I've found out what's wrong with me.' He quickly flicked through the tapering schedule pages and prescribed the diazepam required for me to wean off. I left feeling optimistic. I didn't know how long it was going to take, but I knew I was going to be well again. Not ever having had any type of psychological problem, I dismissed many of the symptoms listed in the *Ashton Manual* as being only likely to occur in people who had anxiety, insomnia or depression as preexisting conditions.

I had no preconceptions of what my withdrawal experience would be like. I devised a quick recovery plan which included stocking up on vitamin Bs, magnesium, calcium, homeopathic tissue salts, melatonin, valerian, taurine, gamma-aminobutyri acid (GABA) and a few other supplements that I thought would help. I was going to accept the symptoms without resistance, give them no attention, speak positively to myself as always, continue meditating twice daily and focus on wellness. I told myself that in a few months I would be fully recovered and would have forgotten about the experience.

When the symptoms started to surface during my first taper attempt I was confident about my ability to cope, but when I started having involuntary seizure-type movements that made driving dangerous, I reinstated in order to be able to go to work. This also happened during my second taper attempt. I eventually gave up work and as a result lost my home. By this time I had already ended my marriage to Dylan. The drug had impacted every area of my life.

As I weaned off the clonazepam during the summer of 2005, the withdrawal symptoms began to surface. Having resolved to accept them without resisting, I did my best to remain calm and assumed the role of 'detached observer'. I felt that if I stayed focused on the fact that the symptoms were indicative of the healing that was taking place, anxiety levels would be kept to a minimum. I would have to cope with the withdrawal-induced issues only.

I continued meditating (although it was difficult during the acute phase when I had the withdrawal-induced agitation), practised mindfulness, used positive self-talk, affirmations, emotional freedom technique (EFT), diaphragmatic breathing and every other coping strategy I was aware of while I witnessed what was happening to my mind and body.

During the acute stage of withdrawal I could not eat or sleep. Every part of my body hurt, tingled, burned and twitched, and my perception was distorted. I was constantly dizzy, my senses were heightened and my eyes were glazed. I had abdominal pains with vomiting, diarrhoea and every other withdrawal symptom conceivable. If I had not had this experience, I would not have believed it possible for a prescribed drug to wreak such havoc. I recall looking in the mirror and thinking I looked like a recreational drug user in detox. At times it was very frightening, but I kept telling myself, 'I am recovering. I am grateful for my healing'.

A few months after my last dose of diazepam, I had a brief period during which the brain fog lifted and some of the symptoms either subsided or lessened in intensity. It was my first glimpse of the long-forgotten mental clarity that would return with recovery. At the time, I thought that withdrawal was over. I was thrilled and immediately started making plans to return to work. The timing was wrong, however, and with my nervous system still in a fragile state, the symptoms quickly returned.

I had another period where the fog again lifted and many of the symptoms relented at six months off. It was soon followed by intense re-emergence of the symptoms. This pattern of intermittent 'waves' of symptoms and welcome 'windows' of clarity continued, with the waves gradually becoming shorter and the windows lasting longer. My tolerance withdrawal began intensifying around 2000 and my taper-related withdrawal period ended in early 2008. For much of this time, apart from having to cope with the waves of dizziness, nausea and other symptoms, my memory was badly impaired. I kept a notebook with my address, telephone number, national insurance (social security) number, the day the rubbish was collected and other important information. I felt like someone suffering from early-onset dementia.

Having kept diaries and journals since my early teens, it was surprisingly easy for me to write during withdrawal. At times it was all I could do. During one of those periods when the symptoms subsided, I started writing about my experience on the Internet. This evolved into the *Benzo-Wise* website, which is now *Recovery Road*, providing comprehensive information, empowerment and coping tools to thousands experiencing withdrawal.

As my memory and other cognitive faculties improved and my clarity sharpened, I began to realize that I was much more unwell during the tolerance years than I had first thought. This is the reason I am extremely thankful that I am now medication-free. To have my cognitive faculties back was worth every minute of withdrawal. I no longer have withdrawal symptoms and am now fully recovered. I do have the pre-existing dystonia which I have had since childhood, but all problems related to withdrawal have disappeared and life is back to normal. I am still in awe of how resilient and self-healing our bodies are. To go from not being able to read or complete a sentence to writing an entire book that people actually want to read is proof of this.

Enduring a challenging and protracted withdrawal can be most empowering. I genuinely believe that having survived withdrawal, I will undauntedly face future life obstacles and so I revel in this new sense of near-invincibility.

The bonus for me has been the privilege of being able to help others in withdrawal. It is by far the most fulfilling and rewarding thing I have ever done and certainly affirms that good can result from a difficult situation. There is a 'preciousness' about life now. I am mostly content and find pleasure in simplicity. I take nothing for granted and am much more aware and appreciative than I was before. These are special gifts which I treasure. Sometimes we are sent unexpected challenges; somehow we find the strength and courage required to cope. We can even learn a few life lessons along the way. I am grateful for my recovery and pleased that life is good again.

2 HOW THEY WORK

When *Recovery Road* was first started, the number of people who contacted us about trying to discontinue both an antidepressant and a tranquilliser was surprising. Somehow we expected it would be one or the other with very few taking both. It was interesting that many were first prescribed the tranquilliser, which is a depressant, then the mood-enhancing antidepressant to deal with side effects. Others were prescribed the antidepressant first, then a tranquilliser to deal with non-efficacy of the drug or the side effects. There were other scenarios but these were the most common. This chapter gives an overview of how antidepressants, sleeping pills and other benzodiazepine tranquillisers work. Because of the common withdrawal-induced cognitive problems that affect information processing, I have not included scientific details that may require your focus and comprehension.

ANTIDEPRESSANTS

No one knows the real answer to the question of how antidepressants work – at least not yet, but extensive research continues. They are primarily used to relieve the symptoms of moderate to severe depression but are also prescribed for other conditions including obsessive-compulsive disorder (OCD), anxiety and eating disorders, migraines, menopause, pre-menstrual tension and chronic pain.

Although how they work is not exactly known, they are believed to increase the activity of certain chemicals in the brain. These chemicals are called neurotransmitters and they function as messengers, used by the nerve cells (or neurons) to communicate with each other. Researchers believe that the neurotransmitters which play a significant role in depression are serotonin, noradrenaline (norepinephrine) and dopamine. They have varying effects including influencing mood, behaviour, learning, emotion, sleep, appetite, heart rate, blood pressure, blood sugar, memory, pleasure and desire.

To send messages, the neurons release neurotransmitters into the spaces between neurons called synapses. These neurotransmitters bind to receiving units or receptors. They increase the amount of neurotransmitters in the brain by blocking their re-uptake and reabsorption into the nerve cells that released them, thus prolonging their effect. There are different types of antidepressants which work in different ways, but most are based on this principle.

The main types of antidepressants are selective serotonin re-uptake inhibitors (SSRIs), serotonin and noradrenaline re-uptake inhibitors (SNRIs), tricyclics (TCAs) and the noradrenaline-specific serotoninergic antidepressants (NaSSAs), which do not work as serotonin re-uptake inhibitors. Monoamine oxidase inhibitors, which, like the NaSSAs, work differently and have numerous drug interactions, have been rarely prescribed in recent times and are not considered here.

When antidepressant treatment commences, the patient is advised to allow at least a month for the therapeutic effects to become evident. It is believed that this is the time it takes for their brain cells to adapt; however, side effects may occur sooner. The most commonly prescribed types of antidepressants used by our helpline callers are SSRIs, SNRIs and TCAs.

SLEEPING PILLS AND OTHER BENZODIAZEPINES

'Be careful. These pills will fry your brain', whispered the wise, white-haired pharmacist as he handed me my final bottle of little beige pills – words I wished I had heard when I filled my first prescription. He did not know I was tapering after having taken them for more than seven years, and that although my brain was not 'fried', my GABA receptors were badly in need of repair.

Some benzodiazepines are widely and successfully used in certain settings, such as in hospitals as pre-medication before operations, as one-off treatment only for nervous patients before a dental procedure, and in the treatment of some forms of epilepsy and movement disorders. They are also used in the management of alcohol withdrawal. They work by enhancing the activity of the neurotransmitter, GABA, which is the most important and widespread messenger in the brain. When benzodiazepines bind to the benzodiazepine sites on the GABA receptors they increase GABA's efficiency and cause a calming effect. There are different receptor subtypes, and with selectivity they cause varying effects: sedation/hypnotic (sleep inducing), anxiolytic (anti-anxiety), muscle relaxant, anticonvulsant and amnesiac (memory disruption).

GABA is an inhibitory neurotransmitter, calming or slowing down the nervous system like the brakes function in a car. There are other neurotransmitters in the brain such as norepinephrine (noradrenaline), dopamine, serotonin, glutamate and acetylcholine. Excitatory neurotransmitters like glutamate function like a car's accelerator. While GABA's inhibitory activity is being enhanced, the activity of other neurotransmitters – some of which are necessary for many essential functions including heart rate and blood pressure control, normal alertness, memory and emotional responses – is affected.

The British National Formulary (BNF), which is a joint publication of the British Medical Association and the Royal Pharmaceutical Society of Great Britain, recommends only short-term (2–4 weeks) use of benzodiazepines in the treatment of anxiety disorders. It also states that the use of benzodiazepines for mild anxiety is inappropriate and unsuitable.

DOWN-REGULATION

In the cases of both antidepressants and benzodiazepines, the longer the drug is taken, the more the receptors change to accommodate the raised levels of neurotransmitters. They become less sensitive or 'down-regulated' and remain this way during the time of usage. When the drug is discontinued, the cells then take time to readapt to the changes or 'up-regulate'. During this period of readjustment withdrawal symptoms can be experienced. The temporary damage or compromised brain mentioned throughout the book refers to this down-regulated state of the receptors.

TOLERANCE

When the receptors in the brain adapt or become habituated to the action of the drug, more is needed in order for the desired therapeutic effect to be achieved. This often develops with regular, long-term use and is known as tolerance. As tolerance sets in, physical dependency occurs and withdrawal symptoms usually then appear.

With addictive substances there is a need to keep increasing dosage because of this tolerance. A good example is the use of alcohol where a new drinker is able to feel an effect after one or two glasses but eventually, as tolerance sets in, will need increasing amounts. In the case of sleeping pills and other benzodiazepines, and with some antidepressants, successive increases in dosage may be periodically needed in order for the required effect to be maintained. Tolerance develops more rapidly with drugs with a short half-life and can lead to additional drugs being prescribed when a safe maximum dose of the one being taken is no longer effective.

HALF-LIFE

There is an ongoing process of drug absorption and elimination when these drugs are taken on a regular basis. The time it takes for half of the drug to be eliminated or for the blood concentration level to fall by half is known as the half-life. This may vary according to the individual, particularly in the elderly.

When someone on a longer-acting half-life drug misses several doses or abruptly discontinues the drug, it can take days before withdrawal symptoms surface. This is important to know as some people who stop taking the medication abruptly spend a brief period thinking that they will not have withdrawal symptoms only to be unpleasantly surprised days or even weeks later.

For example, the half-life of the benzodiazepine, clonazepam, is approximately 18–50 hours. This means that if the last dose was taken at 8:00 a.m. on Monday, it could take up to 10:00 a.m. on Wednesday (50 hours) for half of the drug to be eliminated and possibly another two or more days before withdrawal symptoms are experienced. This is why when I first developed a tolerance to the clonazepam and stopped taking it, the withdrawal-related intense involuntary movements did not surface until three days later.

On the other hand, with a drug like the antidepressant venlafaxine, which has a very short half-life of approximately five hours, within 24 hours most of it is eliminated. Because of this short half-life, withdrawal symptoms can be experienced within hours of missing a dose. Withdrawal problems can also be experienced if the drug has a short half-life and is taken on alternate days when tapering. People who use their medication sporadically or those who take the ones with a short half-life can experience inter-dose withdrawal. When this happens, they begin to feel withdrawal effects between doses. Tapering off a drug with a short half-life by taking it every other day is not advisable as it can intensify the withdrawal process.

PARADOXICAL REACTION

If a patient responds to medication in a contradictory or opposite way to what is expected, it is said to have had a paradoxical effect. An example of this is pain relief medication causing increased pain. Antidepressant treatment can result in the pre-existing condition intensifying so that the person ends up becoming suicidal, severely agitated, hostile, etc. Benzodiazepine treatment, too, can sometimes result in paradoxical reactions in susceptible individuals, causing an increase in anxiety, agitation, aggressiveness, hyperactivity, insomnia and exacerbation of seizures in epileptics.

DEPENDENCY OR ADDICTION?

Although antidepressants and benzodiazepines are taken by illicit drug users, there are tens of thousands of people who have become dependent on them as a result of medical treatment (termed iatrogenic addiction) and who are uncomfortable with being called an 'addict' or 'substance misuser'. This is understandable as the drugs are prescribed for a medical or psychological condition by a doctor. Most have no history of addiction and do not experience cravings. Furthermore, they are often the ones who broach the issue of discontinuing the drug with their doctors.

A theory exists that individuals who experience troubling symptoms or end up with protracted withdrawal syndrome all had addictive tendencies. It claims they were predisposed to addiction – genetically or otherwise – and that this explains their difficulties in coming off the drug. But this is contradicted by the overwhelming anecdotal evidence, which confirms that those with these seemingly extreme withdrawal reactions (usually due to detox or cold-turkey/abrupt discontinuation), when reinstated on the drug and tapered off slowly, quite often end up with fewer symptoms and a less intense experience.

Conversely, there are individuals with a history of addiction who discontinue a benzo or antidepressant with no problems whatsoever. When considering the difficulties of withdrawal, it is mainly the shock to the nervous system through inappropriate and dangerous tapering methods, such as detox and abrupt discontinuation, rather than an addictive tendency or predisposition that appears to be the major contributory factor.

Regardless of opinions or terms used, the reality is that someone who feels compelled to continue taking these drugs often fears the troubling withdrawal symptoms or has a belief that the drug is helping in some way. Because of the connotations and unfortunate stigmatization associated with the word 'addict', the World Health Organization recommends 'dependency' as the expression of choice for people iatrogenically addicted to drugs.

3 THE BASICS

Even people who were usually trusting of my judgement and cared deeply were sceptical about a prescribed drug having such adverse effects. Only after I recovered did they acquiesce with bewilderment and relief. This inability to grasp the complexity and possible duration of withdrawal could be referred to as the 'unbelievability factor'.

If you are experiencing protracted withdrawal and your family, friends or carers insist it is not possible and that withdrawal does not last longer than a few months, please share relevant information from credible sources with them. Then consider your circumstances carefully before doubting yourself or coming to this conclusion. If you do, you could end up feeling that your symptoms are caused by some other medical condition or by the pre-existing problem which withdrawal mimics. This could result in your being misdiagnosed and treated for something that is merely a withdrawal symptom – one which will eventually disappear.

Should you be concerned about the level of physical discomfort you are experiencing, it is advisable to see your doctor and even have diagnostic tests if necessary. The results are usually negative and you will be assured that your symptom is indeed due to withdrawal.

Another way of identifying withdrawal symptoms is that they would first have appeared either during tolerance when the drug stopped being effective, when you first started weaning off, or during or after your taper. Users of medication with very short half-lives and those who take them erratically may also experience symptoms as part of inter-dose withdrawal. You may also find that the symptoms abate during your windows of clarity and resurface during the waves of withdrawal, often with other accompanying symptoms.

I was fortunate that when I observed my psychological symptoms I knew they were caused by nothing more than a nervous system that was temporarily in a state of chaos. I did not focus on the peculiar distortions and waited until after they subsided before mentioning them. I felt I would be at risk of being misdiagnosed with a mental health disorder.

If the furniture or floor appears to be moving or you experience any other bizarre form of distorted perception (which first surfaced during withdrawal), please wait until your recovery process is complete before considering psychiatric treatment. This is provided you feel emotionally safe and are not suicidal. If you are able to regard the distortion as just another withdrawal symptom as you would the gastric disturbances, headaches and other physical symptoms, you will cope. Once you are able to maintain awareness and discernment while observing the symptom, knowing that it is impossible for your furniture to move unaided, you will manage well.

I certainly understand why anyone who has not experienced withdrawal would have doubts. I recall my bewilderment when I first observed the acute symptoms, especially the distorted perception. I used to shake my head in disbelief and fascination thinking how absolutely incredible it was. Later, when I was becoming frustrated at the insistence of everyone, including doctors, that 'It could not possibly still be withdrawal', I reminded myself of how dubious I, too, had been.

There is definitely an 'unbelievability factor' to the withdrawal phenomenon. It is complex and can be a conundrum even to the person in the throes of the experience. If your symptoms are persistent, please keep reminding yourself that although withdrawal can last months or more, it is temporary. While you wait for your nervous system to recover, try to find ways to nurture yourself and get the support you need. In this case, time really does heal. One day you will be well again.

'COLD TURKEY'

The natural inclination once the drug's unwanted effects are identified is to want to stop taking it immediately. This is referred to as quitting 'cold turkey'. One of the most frequently asked questions is whether or not taking this route is advisable. The answer is always an unhesitatingly gentle but firm, 'No'. Abrupt discontinuance of an antidepressant, sleeping pill or other benzo tranquilliser is dangerous and not worth the risk. Even a drastic reduction in dose can result in acute withdrawal reactions.

Some people think that if they stop cold turkey they will avoid the long, unpleasant withdrawal associated with a slow taper. To the contrary, anecdotal evidence suggests that cold-turkey withdrawal is more likely to result in protracted withdrawal than tapering slowly. An abrupt or rushed withdrawal can also cause seizures, withdrawal psychosis and other serious problems. As mentioned earlier, when I realized the medication was no longer effective I threw it away only to find myself convulsing quite intensely about three days later. This stopped once I reinstated. It is a classic example of what can happen if the drug is discontinued abruptly.

Many of the people who contact us have been subject to severe symptoms for unanticipated longer periods and this is the case because, unfortunately, they were taken off their medication abruptly or detoxed off large doses using a rushed tapering protocol. The consensus is that it is advisable and much safer to do a slow taper to give your brain time to readjust to the reductions. For anyone wanting to discontinue an antidepressant, sleeping pill or other benzo tranquilliser, please wean off slowly and have your doctor supervise your taper.

TAPERING

If you are taking both a benzodiazepine and antidepressant, withdrawing from the benzodiazepine first is usually recommended. It is very important to again note that antidepressant withdrawal can be just as intense as benzodiazepine withdrawal and so they need to be tapered off safely too.

There are different recommended methods for tapering, some of which are successfully used. For anyone who has taken the drug long-term, it is advisable to not rush the process. The schedules must be flexible and reduction rate should be based on withdrawal reactions and intensity of symptoms. For short-term users, tapering over very long periods will prolong the period in which the receptors remain down-regulated.

The *Ashton Manual* recommends the use of diazepam (Valium) to taper off other benzodiazepines because it is eliminated from the body more slowly. Diazepam comes in liquid form and in doses of 10 mg, 5 mg and 2 mg, which makes it easy to make very minute reductions in doses.

If you have decided to discontinue taking your medication, there are a few factors which will determine the duration and pace of your taper and how well you are likely to cope:

- If you are on a high dose, you will take longer to withdraw. The drug will be reduced in very small increments periodically in order to allow your body to readjust to the new doses at each stage of reduction.

- The tapering schedule should be used only as a guide. If you require a longer period to taper, you can discuss this with your doctor and adjust it accordingly.

- Many people use razor blades or the milk or water titration method to make the smallest possible cuts. It is believed that the smaller the cut, the gentler it is and the easier it will be for your central nervous system to adjust.

- Drugs differ in potency. If you are on a highly potent one you will need a longer time to reduce.

- Your personal circumstances, overall general health, the stressors in your life, stamina, support available and previous experience with drugs, if any, may also influence how you cope and determine the pace at which you can realistically taper.

If you are faced with additional stress, such as a bereavement, admission to hospital or other crisis while tapering, it is acceptable and in some cases necessary to remain on the same stage of the withdrawal for a longer period. It is also important to avoid increasing the dose at this time, if possible. Once your circumstances are more settled, a further reduction in dose can be made.

You will need the cooperation of your doctor. If using the substitution or any other method, she or he will also be prescribing the medication required and will also be supervising your taper.

Having a support system in place is best. It would be good if you had a reliable family member or friend who is willing to learn about your medication and withdrawal. It is extremely important that you set the pace for your taper and not feel rushed to complete it or have anyone pressure you into weaning off quicker than what is comfortable for you. This time *you* are in charge.

If you have received conflicting advice about tapering, don't let this confuse you. Despite claims that some tapering protocols are more successful than others, people who have used similar methods can have varying results, ranging from good to challenging. The worst accounts are from those who either stopped abruptly or rushed their tapers. But once you wean off gently and slowly under medical supervision, decide the pace at which you will proceed and keep the mindset that you can and will succeed, you will find that coming off your medication is attainable. You can do it.

RECOVERY TIMELINE

The average time recovery takes for those coming off sleeping pills and other tranquillisers is currently regarded to be between 6 and 18 months. Those with milder dependencies can take as little as 1–6 weeks. This is not always the case, however, because the withdrawal experience is unique and varies according to the individual. This is why no one knows or can accurately predict how long it will take. We have not noticed any differences between timelines for antidepressants and benzodiazepines. Depending on the degree of dependency, antidepressant withdrawal can be just as challenging with similar duration as tranquilliser withdrawal.

Dosage and number of years a person has been taking the drug are sometimes considered to be good indicators. Anecdotal evidence shows that there is a tendency for those who have been on high doses for many years to experience a longer withdrawal period than shorter-term users. Still, it is useful to note that a person on a low dose for months and one on a high dose for years can end up having quite similar experiences. All the doctors I consulted during withdrawal insisted it does not last for more than a few weeks, 6 months at most. They were misinformed. Weeks, months or years, withdrawal takes as long as the nervous system needs to complete the repair process.

If your symptoms are many and severe, it does not mean your withdrawal will last longer. Conversely, having fewer and less intense symptoms does not mean your withdrawal period will be shorter. There is just no proven pattern of healing. Also, if you are taking other medication, consuming alcohol, experimenting with supplements that work on the nervous system or over-stimulating and over-exerting yourself, this could affect you.

Windows of clarity appear early to some, but this does not always mean that their withdrawal period will be shorter. I had my first window approximately 8 weeks after completing my taper, but symptoms persisted for two more years.

Some people take a much longer time to have their first window, but this does not mean their withdrawal period will be longer. Others have short, frequent windows which gradually increase in duration until recovery is complete. Some have few or no windows but may take the same or even less time to recover, with symptoms spontaneously and permanently disappearing.

Comparing your situation with that of someone who you know has been on a similar dose and tapering schedule will do more harm than good. Our bodies respond differently. Another important reason is that, although you may have been on similar doses with the same tapering schedules and methods, you may not know the person's full circumstances. She or he may have less support, could have a pre-existing condition, be taking other medication, consuming alcohol, trying different complementary therapies, taking supplements or over-stimulating in some other way of which you are unaware.

You may also encounter well-meaning friends who announce that certain supplements, forms of therapy or rigorous exercise programmes miraculously accelerated their healing. Before you embark on a similar regimen or approach, please remember how individual a process recovery is. For every 'remedy' that has supposedly helped someone, you will find others who have said it caused their symptoms to worsen. I still find this quite remarkable, but it is true.

There will always be this element of contradiction. To attribute one's healing, or symptoms for that matter, to anything specific will be debatable until formal research is done. How can we tell? You could start taking a supplement just at the time when improvements were imminent anyway, or when a flare-up was poised to surface. Speculation does not help. There are too many varying conditions to come to conclusions. If you feel that whatever is recommended is worth trying, be optimistic but remain open to the fact that a different outcome is possible.

Finally, no one can predict how long it will take to recover or how the process will unfold. What we do know is that managing withdrawal requires large doses of patience, non-resistance and the wise application of coping techniques. These will certainly make the time seem shorter.

If the process is taking longer than anticipated, it is because your resilient nervous system needs more time to recover. Think of the many people before you (including me) who made it through to recovery despite how troubling the symptoms were or how long they lasted. You will too. Even if you tapered too quickly and think you've made a mistake, don't worry. Our bodies are remarkably self-healing. Just keep believing that you are going to get better. Keep holding on. You will make it to recovery. When the timing is right for you, this chapter will end and you will be able to move on and resume a normal life.

4   SYMPTOMS

This chapter on symptoms is relevant whether you are coming off an antidepressant, sleeping pill or other benzo tranquilliser, or a similar-acting Z-drug. As mentioned previously, the symptoms experienced are very similar. At *Recovery Road* we have noticed subtle differences that may be coincidental but which will be mentioned here. We have found that some coming off antidepressants experience what they describe as severe agitation or akathisia, flu-like symptoms, suicidal ideation and varying sensory sensations such as burning, zaps, buzzing, waves and electric-like shocks, to a greater extent than our clients who used tranquillisers only. Please note that this is just our anecdotal observation and has no scientific basis whatsoever.

Because the symptoms can be baffling, complex, unpredictable and persistent, they sometimes steal our focus away from recovery. It is easy to become fixated and spend many hours browsing for information, analyses and diagnoses. There were times when I had to drag myself away from my computer for fear of developing 'cyberchondria'. Too much information about symptoms can be overwhelming and may cause additional anxiety.

It is because of this tendency that I have limited the content of this chapter and will give only a brief overview. The comprehensive A to Z list of reported symptoms, which can be seen at the back of the book, and the detailed journal entries throughout, provide adequate and more in-depth information.

Despite being aware that the emergence of withdrawal symptoms in someone who has been taking an antidepressant or tranquilliser long-term is a natural response to discontinuance, dosage reduction or tolerance, it does not prevent distress when they appear. Even the strongest of characters may become apprehensive. A pragmatic way of dealing with intermittent waves or flare-ups is to regard every single symptom as being present only because the nervous system is in temporary overdrive. It is the long-term use of the drug that has caused temporary, reversible changes to the brain. Accepting that a myriad of symptoms may be present in varying degrees of intensity until the affected receptors are repaired will help significantly with coping.

For many in withdrawal, one of the most challenging aspects is determining whether some of the bizarre things that happen to the mind and body are symptoms or dreaded diseases. Although I thought I was well informed about withdrawal symptoms, when I first had my perception distorted I was concerned. It was scary and I felt unprepared. Only after doing more research and finding further supporting evidence did I accept it. Receiving confirmation that the strange occurrences are indeed symptoms provides relief and reassurance. This is one of the reasons the websites and online groups are so well utilized.

Please do not allow the following summary of my symptoms to deter you. They were experienced in clusters, and although at the time I felt as if my transition to the non-physical was imminent, I now think of them with non-egoistic pride that I coped so well. Since they are only symptoms and were all due to withdrawal, I have not analysed them or linked them to any diagnoses. Despite the fact that they mimic common medical and psychological conditions, they are, in this case, part of the withdrawal syndrome.

The most important thing while you read this is to keep reminding yourself that not everyone will experience all or many of them. For those who do, they may be less intense and last for a short period, usually during the acute phase. Remember, the reason you don't hear from the people who had very few or no symptoms is because they may not even have consulted the Internet. They are busy living their lives. Some are clueless as to how fortunate they were.

Here are the symptoms I experienced: headaches, tight band around head, distorted visual, auditory and tactile perception manifesting in bizarre ways, muscle pain, burning, profuse sweating, intrusive thoughts, spasms and other involuntary muscle movements, gastrointestinal disturbances, sleep difficulty with nightmares, benzo belly, lethargy, skin rashes, heart irregularities, mouth and teeth pain, light and sound hypersensitivity, dizziness, tinnitus and various other anxiety-related problems.

A significant number of these symptoms were experienced during the acute withdrawal period and gradually disappeared. Withdrawal really does become a distant memory. If I had not journalized my symptoms, I would not be able to write about them now. I recall attributing everything that happened from the beginning of my taper to my recovery as being withdrawal related. If I had lost an eyelash during that time I would have said, 'Wow! Loss of eyelash is another symptom.' No, please don't check your lashes; it is not.

If in any doubt about a symptom, please seek medical advice. It is important to not allow this withdrawal experience to make you hyper-vigilant or paranoid about receiving medical care. When my left hand and fingers became numb, I had diagnostic tests to rule out other causes. They were all negative and confirmed that it was withdrawal. I was not surprised when the numbness eventually went away and my hand returned to normal.

Consulting a doctor who is knowledgeable about antidepressants and benzodiazepines will reduce the probability of your being misdiagnosed. Even if your doctor is hesitant, what you may notice is that you gradually become accustomed to the symptoms and will be able to easily identify them as being withdrawal related.

WITHDRAWAL OR UNDERLYING ISSUE?

'How do I know if what is happening is really due to withdrawal?' This is a most frequently asked question. The problem stems from being told one could not possibly still be in withdrawal and that the pre-existing condition has returned or some new medical or psychological condition has developed. Doubts are also due to the symptoms mimicking a past problem: 'My husband says as far back as he can remember I have been a very anxious person.'

To distinguish between withdrawal and other issues or return of an underlying condition, we have found the following to be most useful:

- *Diagnostics.* Results of tests will usually be negative. There are a few that may not be normal, but this will still be due to withdrawal. For example, blood sugar and blood pressure could be high or low, an electroencephalography of the brain may show slightly abnormal electrical activity and/or an electrocardiogram could show mild heart irregularities, but these will be withdrawal reactions. Also, many people are nutrient-deficient in withdrawal (due to not being able to take vitamins/supplements or from having modified diets) so certain levels may be low.

- *Timing.* If the symptom surfaced during or after your taper, or even while you were on the drug (but were most likely in tolerance withdrawal – when a dosage increase is needed in order for it to be effective) it can be regarded as withdrawal related.

- *Medical/physical symptoms.* If it is a psychological symptom, are medical symptoms present as well? Usually they are, and they would have appeared around the same time. But even if you have no medical symptoms, once you are within the usual withdrawal time frame, it is best to wait before considering other treatment. Provided you are emotionally safe and able to cope, waiting is the wisest option.

• *Reinstatement.* A reliable way of confirming a withdrawal-related symptom is if it dramatically disappeared after you took the drug again. Of course, you won't be doing this to check. (If you are well into your recovery and are coping, reinstating is not advisable. If you are having seizures, psychosis, etc., due to a cold-turkey or detox situation, then yes, see your doctor immediately regarding reinstating.)

• *'Chemical' feel.* Many of our callers say they can tell the difference and that the withdrawal-related symptoms feel 'chemical' or organic – caused by the imbalances created by the drug. They describe this 'chemical' feel as more of a strange physical feeling which involves adrenaline rushes, shakiness, agitation, lethargy, etc., accompanied by the most intense organic fear/anxiety or depression with no apparent emotional link. They usually describe it as being 'off the charts' and nothing like what they used to feel before withdrawal.

ACCEPTANCE

Ample references regarding the importance of non-resistance are made throughout this book in order to normalize what is happening. This is because acceptance is the most important requirement for efficiently managing withdrawal. To resolve to cope successfully without fully accepting the presence of the symptoms is unrealistic.

For some people, acceptance implies giving up, resignation or failure. In your world, however, acceptance means less distress and minimal anxiety. It is the difference between barely surviving withdrawal and coping well. Imagine that you are on your way home. You know without doubt that you will arrive. You look ahead and notice there is a massive traffic jam. You are stuck. There is no way out but through. All you can do is resign yourself to waiting. This is withdrawal.

If you can apply the same approach to your symptoms, you will fare much better than if you try to direct or control how your recovery process unfolds. As you become aware of your symptoms, try to go with the feelings without struggling or attempting to stop them. You may not be able to do this easily at first, but as you learn to observe your body's physiological reactions, you will find that you can make a mental note of what is happening without letting the fear overcome you. Even if your anxiety levels are extremely high, you can simply surrender; resolve to do nothing but be with the feeling of your hands shaking, heart beating fast, agitation or however it manifests.

Whenever I had an intense feeling of fear or impending doom, I would take deep breaths and talk myself through it without resisting: 'Okay, here we go again; it's back. Ah well, at least I know what it is. Hmm… Feels like I'm petrified but I'm not really. Gosh, look how shaky I am. This is normal. I don't need to do anything. I know what it is and it will soon pass.' It works; just don't fight it.

You are not going to stop breathing, faint, fall or die as much as it may feel that way. When you think that as intense as the feeling is, you have had it before and it has never caused any harm. Whatever you feared might happen, did not. You can use this to reassure yourself that as terrified as you may be feeling while it is happening, you are going to be okay. Breathe and repeat. It can take time and practice to become fully accepting. You may occasionally still resist the symptoms. This is normal as it is instinctive behaviour to struggle when a threat is perceived. The key is to not give up or become impatient with yourself when this happens.

Try to see your symptoms as little inconveniences – the cars ahead of you in the traffic. You will soon notice that even if at first you do give in and fight a particular symptom, with practice you will eventually be able to choose how you respond. Yes, you are stuck with annoying and sometimes frightening symptoms, but it is only a temporary setback. You will make it home to recovery.

Withdrawal is literally healing in action. If you are able to acknowledge each symptom, no matter how disturbing, as necessary – evidence that your nervous system is recovering – you will be able to truly accept them. As some say when new symptoms appear or old ones resurface: 'So this is what it feels like to heal.'

5 MANAGING PSYCHOLOGICAL SYMPTOMS

The physical symptoms, no matter how unbearable, are often less frightening than the psychological. If a person has a bloated, distended stomach which is sometimes painful (benzo belly), there are certain things that will be done intuitively to cope. Without giving it much thought, he or she may decide to wear loose or elasticated waist clothing and avoid wheat. Coping with the disconcerting psychological symptoms, however, is another matter.

Many people in withdrawal consider coping with the psychological symptoms to be more difficult. They find them distressing and regard them differently to the physical symptoms. Not resisting is understandably more challenging. If you are experiencing psychological symptoms, here is relevant information along with a few thoughts and suggestions which I hope will be useful.

BRAIN FOG

Brain fog is the term used to describe cognitive dysfunction which causes feelings of mental confusion and lack of mental clarity. It is associated with difficulty concentrating or learning new things, problems with reading comprehension and memory impairment. Statements used to describe this symptom include:

'I feel like my head is enveloped in a thick cloud.'

'I used to be good at getting my point across; now I can't complete my sentences.'

'I can't figure out simple instructions.'

'I think one word but say another.'

'I feel like I'm lost in a dense fog.'

Brain fog is one of the reasons many people in withdrawal are misdiagnosed. This could be due to the fact that it is also common in other conditions including chronic fatigue syndrome and fibromyalgia. It is also a symptom of heavy-metal poisoning, and one of the first things I did when I was feeling unwell but had not yet identified the drug as the culprit was to have my dentist remove all my amalgam (mercury-containing) fillings. They were replaced with composite ones, but this did not make a difference. I don't regret having had the dental work done, but to treat brain fog, the underlying condition has to be corrected. In our case it is withdrawal syndrome due to down-regulation of our receptors, and time is the only cure of which we are aware.

Attempting to accomplish simple tasks when coping with brain fog can be frustrating. As you wait for the recovery process to be completed, acknowledge that your limitations are temporary and try not to force yourself or struggle to do more than that of which you are capable. You will benefit, though, from gently stimulating your brain by using word games, puzzles or reading a simple book. Keep a notebook to record relevant information, journalize your thoughts if you feel up to it and find your best or peak time to do things that require concentration.

Brain fog was one of my most persistent symptoms. I remember in moments of doubt, wondering whether it would ever go. As I neared the end of withdrawal my clarity improved remarkably. Had I not kept a journal, I would now have very limited recollection of what life was like with a foggy brain.

DEPERSONALIZATION

With depersonalization comes a sense of detachment and disconnection, as if the person is an outside observer of his or her body or mental processes. Statements used to describe this symptom include:

'I feel like an alien in my own body.'

'I feel detached, in an unfamiliar space.'

'I feel lifeless, mechanical, foreign...'

'I feel as if I am observing myself acting a part in the movie of my surreal life.'

This depersonalization experienced during withdrawal is not present because of a dissociative disorder or any other psychological illness, so please be assured. It is withdrawal induced and, in that sense, is no different from muscle and joint pain, skin problems or any other physical symptom. As the nervous system begins to recover, the depersonalization usually becomes less intense and eventually fades away. In some cases it goes spontaneously. It can be intense one day and completely gone the next.

One way of accepting this symptom can be to regard it as an important self-protecting tool. When you think about the stressors and psychological trauma that some are subject to during withdrawal, it would make sense that being detached and emotionless may in the most unlikely way lessen the impact.

DEREALIZATION

Derealization causes one's perception to be altered, resulting in a sense of being in a strange or 'unreal' reality. Statements used to describe this symptom include:

'I feel a lack of emotional depth.'

'I feel an inability to be spontaneous.'

'I feel as if I am observing everyone and everything around me through a thick, hazy veil.'

'I feel distant, cut off, spaced out and withdrawn from the world.'

'I feel as if I am in a dream, an almost trance-like state in an unfamiliar world.'

Like depersonalization, this is a withdrawal symptom and nothing more. It does not need to be analysed or treated as one would in the case of a dissociative or other mental health disorder. Again, reminding yourself that it is a result of your discontinuing the antidepressant or benzo, and that you should regard it in the same manner as you would one of your physical symptoms, will lessen any related anxiety. You may benefit from using mindfulness positive self-talk and grounding exercises to cope with both the depersonalization and derealization.

DEPRESSIVE THOUGHTS OR LOW MOODS

I hesitate to use the term 'depression' to describe the feelings of helplessness, hopelessness, sadness, social withdrawal, lack of enjoyment in activities and other issues that are present in some people who experience a difficult and protracted withdrawal. This is because it is better to normalize and accept these feelings, which are a combination of an organic reaction due to discontinuance of the drug and having to cope with the repercussions. Directly or indirectly, they are present as a result of withdrawal. But if you do think you are depressed, that's okay too. Whatever the terminology used, it is a normal reaction to having to endure such intense symptoms, emotional numbness and feelings of disconnectedness.

When these moods of hopelessness are overwhelming, there is an inability to conceive a positive thought, be motivated or be proactive. This is when talking to someone about your feelings can help. A phone call to a helpline may assist in lightening your mood. You do not need to explain about withdrawal or justify why you feel the way you do; a good helpline worker will listen actively and without judgement. If you have the support of family or friends, you could share how you feel and ask that someone check in with you regularly. Counselling sessions with a therapist who understands the withdrawal process can also be useful.

Interacting with nature can be beneficial too, and you may find going for walks or a gentle swim to be uplifting. External aids are valuable at this time and some people have found that although there is an inability to genuinely elicit a positive feeling, it can be triggered by a motivational or relaxation CD, podcast or book.

PARANOID IDEATION

Another bizarre symptom of withdrawal is a preoccupation with unfounded, suspicious thoughts. The person may read negative meanings into innocent remarks, perceive some form of threat or persecution, or have delusions that others are plotting against him or her. There is an expectation of being harmed or exploited and the person is hypersensitive to any form of criticism. Usually this symptom is not as intense in someone in withdrawal as it is with a genuine paranoid-schizophrenic case, but it can still be a source of worry.

As is the case with the other psychological symptoms, these paranoid thoughts will disappear when the neurological balances are re-established. Accepting that the symptom is present and that it is a result of temporary changes in the brain can help with coping. Also, being able to detach and observe any thoughts of perceived threats while acknowledging that they are irrational should prevent inappropriate retaliatory behaviour.

OBSESSIVE, UNWANTED THOUGHTS

This can be the most distressing symptom for some, especially in cases where the thoughts are frightening – about death and disasters, or of a sexually taboo nature. I am aware of individuals who were told they had OCD only to later confirm that it was just a withdrawal symptom. The thoughts were induced by the reversible receptor damage – triggered by temporary neurological imbalances – and faded as recovery progressed without medication or other treatment.

Despite knowing that an obsessive, unwanted thought has surfaced because of withdrawal, it can be difficult to accept it and not resist. Because it invades the mind and crowds out other thoughts, it can be very upsetting. Fighting the thoughts will not cause them to go away; attaching additional fear to the idea of having them or to their content will intensify them. Accepting them as a symptom and acknowledging they are false is the first step. Then comes the mantra: 'This is due to withdrawal; it's not me.'

Some people use what is known as the 'thought-stopping process' where they say a firm 'stop' in their heads and distract themselves with an activity such as a puzzle or word game. They do this to interrupt the obsessive process, not to stop thinking, and so there is no resistance. Others simply refocus and, if the thoughts are out of character, switch to another thought: 'I would never choose to have these thoughts; this is all withdrawal related.' They then gently introduce an affirmation or self-talk such as: 'My mind is sound and I am well.'

If you are having obsessive thoughts, try not to give them too much energy. Don't panic or even be surprised when they surface and don't dwell on the content or the fact that it is happening. See if you are able to place them into the same category as you would an upset stomach or any of the other physical symptoms. These thoughts do not last indefinitely. We often hear from individuals who had this symptom and were surprised when it stopped. After, when they access it from memory, they are able to refer to it without having a negative reaction as they did when it was obsessive. They are pleased to discover that the fear is no longer attached to the thought.

'RATIONAL' MIND

When these psychological symptoms persist, many end up with the most troubling thoughts and feelings. They fear that these bizarre symptoms may be permanent. I am always relieved when someone refers to the 'rational' mind. Once I read or hear the words, 'But then my rational mind says it is the drug and not me', I can predict this person will cope more successfully than someone who is unable to make this distinction. Being aware that the thoughts and feelings are present because of withdrawal and are not solely emotional or psychological in origin makes a big difference.

When these thoughts overcrowd the mind, it can be challenging to access a train of rational thought. However, the rational mind is still there; it still exists and is very much intact. When, in the midst of all the fear thoughts, you happen to get an 'I wonder if this is because of my withdrawal?' or similar thought, it is from your rational mind.

Here is where having a prepared monologue of positive self-talk or an affirmation can distract you and save you from immediately drifting back to the fear thoughts. Imagine that you have been struggling with a stream of unwanted thoughts, for example, the dreaded, 'What if my brain is permanently damaged and I never recover?' Then you notice that just one rational thought has eased its way in: 'But this isn't me.' You immediately recognize that you have engaged your rational mind.

If you have your monologue ready, you can use this gap to jump on the rational thought train: 'Yes, these thoughts are not me. I did not have them before withdrawal. They emerged during my taper along with other symptoms. They will go along with all those other symptoms when withdrawal ends. This is definitely due to withdrawal and not me. My mind is sound.' This can be applied to general thoughts of concern about withdrawal or to the more intense obsessive, unwanted ones.

If you are having periods where your mind becomes overcrowded with paranoid or other unwanted thoughts, or your perception is altered, I hope this will work for you. Your rational thought processes, remember, haven't abandoned you permanently. They will return either during the gaps, during your windows of clarity or when withdrawal is over.

Provided you were not having these psychological symptoms prior to withdrawal – whether tolerance withdrawal or withdrawal that commenced with your taper, the reality is that they are due to your discontinuing the drug and not a result of a mental health issue. This is the temporarily compromised, withdrawal brain trying to play tricks with your authentic mind, which is very much still intact. Be reassured that you are in control and you are not losing your mind. It is a temporary, reversible brain issue. Your mind is sound. These thoughts will go.

The best way to cope with psychological symptoms which emerge at the time of tapering off the drug or during any stage of withdrawal is to quickly acknowledge that they are present only because of your temporary receptor damage. Although very distressing, they are common and should be regarded in the same way as you would the physical symptoms. No matter what you are experiencing, always remember that the source of the problem is being repaired (receptors are being up-regulated), and in time, these symptoms will all go. Let this be the spark that ignites the belief and resolve you need to help you stay afloat while you wait.

6 ACUTE WITHDRAWAL

As I share my account with you, I ask that you please take it for what it is: just one person's story. This is not a prediction of what yours will be like. Look out for the tendency to search frantically for stories you feel could be similar to yours, which you think will help you to map out your journey. You have to let go of any need to control the process. You must accept what is happening and trust that your resilient, self-healing nervous system knows exactly what it is doing. Your recovery is inevitable. Just when the timing is right for you, your receptors will complete their up-regulation process and any symptoms you are experiencing will go. So don't let what you are about to read discourage you in any way. I was in tolerance withdrawal for at least four years prior to tapering off the clonazepam and was taken off abruptly (and reinstated) on three occasions prior to my taper. This could be a part of the reason my experience was so challenging.

If you are yet to taper or have just started, please know that your experience could turn out to be much less intense – like the many who have mild withdrawal reactions for a few weeks or months. I am sharing the journals especially for those having distressing symptoms, with the goal of giving you a more uplifting perspective and lighting a candle of hope in your darkest moments.

Acute withdrawal syndrome is reported to last from less than a week to 1 month with a peak at around the second week, in most cases. It can be the most frightening period for anyone in withdrawal, even when warned of the possibility of the physical and psychological symptoms. It is almost as if the nervous system is mourning the loss of the drug and is in a state of shock. Actually, it is.

The first few months after my last dose of clonazepam were the scariest. It was my third attempt at weaning off and I thought I was prepared. As shared before, because I did not have pre-existing anxiety or depression I dismissed the likelihood of my having most of the symptoms mentioned. I was unpleasantly surprised.

I recall not sleeping for four consecutive nights when I neared the end of the clonazepam part of my taper. Apart from the insomnia, my other early symptom was a constant tight band around my head like it was being held in a vice grip, gradually being tightened. Then more symptoms, including the intense involuntary movements, surfaced.

During that first week completely off the clonazepam I took magnesium, calcium, the B vitamins, valerian, melatonin and herbal teas at different times, but nothing worked. I even tried hypnosis and relaxation CDs for sleep. It didn't take long for me to accept that only time could heal the imbalances all those years of benzo use had caused. My nervous system was much too sensitive and in the end I just drank adequate amounts of water and waited it out.

I used every coping technique I was aware of, including positive self-talk, affirmations, EFT and diaphragmatic breathing, as often as I could, and this distracted me and kept me grounded. I knew that what was happening to my body and mind was a result of my discontinuing the drug and considered it to be the beginning of my recovery. As much as I could, I did not allow it to overwhelm me, and although I was scared, I somehow knew I would survive.

The following journal entries were written while I was in Houston, Texas. They give graphic descriptions of my experience around the time I completed the clonazepam part of my taper.

As you read them, again, remember that I was in tolerance withdrawal for many of the eight years that I took the drug. For some of you this phase will only be mildly problematic. You may experience only a few symptoms and with much less intensity.

JOURNAL LOGS

June 29, 2005

THE COUNTDOWN

My taper has been manageable so far. In another two and a half weeks I will be completely off the clonazepam. No matter what happens, there is no way I will be reinstating. If I do, I may as well give up on ever being well again. I want to get my cognitive faculties back. This is all that matters to me now. Just a few more months and I will be completely benzo-free.

I have not been feeling too well this week but I know I will cope. Whatever happens during withdrawal, I am going to be fine. I am not the first person to quit benzos. Those before me recovered. I will too. *I can do this. I will do this. This is the beginning of my healing.*

July 8, 2005

WEEPINESS

For the first time in years, I am beginning to be able to feel again. To have this confirmation that the emotional bluntness is going is encouraging. I cried for most of this week. Luther Vandross died last Friday and Houston's *Sunny 99.1 FM* hosts have been playing his mellow ballads non-stop. I remember seeing him in concert in Maryland almost ten years ago. He was a legend. Every time I hear one of his songs, I burst into tears. It is so sad.

Then I just went online and read that Richard Whitely, the host of 'Countdown', one of my favourite quiz programmes in the UK, recently made his transition. I will miss him too. I didn't personally know him though, so why have I been crying as if I have lost a family member? To make things worse, more than 50 innocent people have died in the UK train bombings. What an atrocity.

This is a breakthrough in my recovery. I noticed earlier, as the tears started flowing, that I could literally feel an unfamiliar tug of my heart strings. After being on the drug for a few years, I forgot what it was like to feel this profoundly.

I know I'm not only crying for Luther, Richard and the UK victims, I am crying for my mother and for every loss that occurred during my emotionally anaesthetized years. These flowing tears are like a rebirth. It feels good to be able to connect with my feelings again. This is my release. I am okay. I will cry until there are no more tears.

July 17, 2005

SCREAMING RECEPTORS

The stomach cramps and loose stools have returned. The pain is excruciating. I feel as if I am going to pass out. I just drank peppermint tea and took two teaspoons of aloe-vera gel. Placebo effect or not, it will go away. I am soaking wet. I haven't stopped perspiring and despite the air conditioning, I look as if I recently showered and forgot to dry myself off.

I am nauseated and have no appetite. My head is pounding and my eyes hurt. They look glassy, like a cocaine addict's. My joints hurt, my muscles ache and my legs feel like jelly; I can hardly stand. I have this crawling, stinging sensation on my skin. This is weird!

All the teeth in my mouth hurt. I have not slept for the last four nights. I can't tolerate light and sounds are exaggerated. My heart beats wildly and echoes in my brain. I am jumpy and my head spins all the time, especially when I stand. Things seem to be moving all around me and my gait is unsteady.

This is scary. Well tough! I won't be taking any more poison. If I didn't understand what was happening to me I would have dialled

911 for an ambulance or checked myself into a hospital or mental health institution by now.

Despite everything, I am happy I know about withdrawal now. All these symptoms are normal according to the research I've done. Every time my stomach cramps or the pain becomes unbearable I affirm: *I am releasing, I am grateful for my healing.*

July 25, 2005

A LITTLE LESS INTENSE

I am lying down as I write this. Today is a little bit better. I slept for two hours last night and I've stopped throwing up. My stomach still gripes and my abdomen is swollen. The band around my head feels tighter and my eyes are glazed and shiny. They look as if they're popping out of my head.

This is scary because when I look in the mirror I'm seeing someone else. I am disconnected, as if this is not me. I feel as if I'm floating and I can only stand for a few minutes. When I do, I feel as if the floor is rising up to meet me.

My skin feels as if insects are crawling all over me, I'm still seeing flashing lights and I'm dripping wet almost all the time. *Okay...calm down...breathe. You know what this is. Your brain is screaming for the drug. That's all it is.*

I feel like phoning 911 for an ambulance but dare not. They will definitely have me confined to a mental health institution. I will not panic. I will lie here and trust that these feelings will soon subside. In time my brain will readjust to this change. I will not give in. I will be brave. This is my healing. *I am safe. My mind is sound.* This is my chance to get my life back.

I endured these intense symptoms for at least another 3 weeks. I found strength, courage and determination that I never knew I had and managed to cope well. It was bewildering at times but I totally surrendered and accepted the symptoms. By this time,

I had very little money left. I could not have afforded another month's rent and so decided to leave Houston.

August 27, 2005

AT SIX WEEKS OFF CLONAZEPAM

Tomorrow I will be leaving for the UK. The hurricane is heading for the Gulf. I hope everyone is safe and that there are no fatalities. Hope it doesn't affect the flights. Don't know how I will cope with the airport chaos but at least I am not vomiting any more.

I liked it here although I was isolated. I guess it was best for me to go through this part of withdrawal on my own. I cannot imagine any of my friends or family seeing me like this and not calling for an ambulance.

I feel totally disconnected and am still wobbly on my feet. I'm still fitting a lot but you know what? I'm going to make it safely home. I have always been divinely guided and protected and this is no exception.

I am grateful for the strength and will to be able to travel safely. Thank you for an incident free journey. *All is well. I am well.*

When I wrote the following log, I was determined to remain optimistic and not get into the victim mode. Withdrawal is so all-consuming and overwhelming, this can easily happen. It is not that the negatives of the experience are being overlooked, it is actually a necessity to not feel helpless and a victim. We have to be valiant and vigilant – at least most of the time. So this log may sound like a lecture, but it is a good example of positive self-talk.

October 8, 2005

ACUTE WITHDRAWAL IS OVER

You have made it safely through acute withdrawal and that proves how strong you are physically and mentally. Remember to say 'well done' and 'thank you'. This chapter is now closed. Today I feel the need to remind you that this is a temporary situation. Do not let your current symptoms consume you and freak you out. Fear will weaken you and right now you need all your strength. I am not saying that you should pretend as if all is well. Actually yes, that is exactly what you need to do. Why? Because acting 'as if' will make you feel better, even if only emotionally. Do what is necessary on a practical level to be comfortable, then take yourself to a mental haven of vibrant health.

You are not a victim and withdrawal is not a 'bad thing' that has happened to you. To the contrary, coming off the drug is the best thing that could have happened. This is what you need to celebrate. This is a blessing and many good experiences await you because of it. You are just unable to see the bigger picture at this time. You can visualize it though. It will keep you focused and this is what you need as your healing takes place, not fear and sadness.

When you write or speak about your symptoms frequently and for long periods you are expanding their influence. You are giving them more energy and power; no wonder you are becoming overwhelmed. You know better; focus on what you want, not what you don't want. View this experience as temporary, which it is, and give the negative aspects as little attention as possible. For every symptom you have, think of wellness. See yourself as you hope to be when you recover. Then you will be less anxious. Because you have changed your focus to all the good that you know awaits you, you become patient and non-resistant as your healing unfolds.

That was quite a severe rant, but I felt I had to take drastic action to avoid depression.

As intense as the acute phase sounds, it *is* manageable. Awareness and acceptance are useful coping tools and it allowed me to observe the symptoms while appreciating that it was the beginning of my recovery process. This was when I acknowledged the usefulness of being able to detach and witness the symptoms, regarding them as being part of the withdrawal syndrome and not individual medical or psychological disorders.

I admit that at times some of the symptoms were frightening. It was the first time I had experienced anxiety or distortion of my perception. But more than anything, I was fascinated by the imbalances that resulted from my discontinuing the drug and the peculiar manifestations. Once the symptoms lessened in intensity, I exhaled. I did not collapse and die. I did not get up in the middle of the night, howling at the moon while running around Texas Medical Center, as I feared I would when I first experienced distortion of my perception. This was an organic reaction and nothing more; my mind was sound and my recovery process was on schedule.

7 POST-ACUTE AND PROTRACTED WITHDRAWAL

Not everyone will experience protracted withdrawal syndrome. Unfortunately, there are some who do. When this happens the tendency is to have a complex process with symptoms which, as we are aware, are the direct result of drug-induced changes to the brain's receptors, as well as the manifestation of indirect effects of long-term use of the drug.

When symptoms persist longer than 18 months the withdrawal is considered to be protracted. Complaints can be as vague as flu-like symptoms or a combination of pathologies mimicking chronic fatigue syndrome, lupus, fibromyalgia, multiple sclerosis, anxiety disorders, irritable bowel syndrome and other chronic conditions.

Common to this phase of withdrawal are periods where the symptoms gradually lessen in intensity or abate totally only to resurface intermittently. As you already know, these recurrences are often referred to as 'waves' and the periods of reprieve as 'windows'.

The following logs were written during my post-acute and protracted periods. At the time of writing the first entry, I did not understand the concept of waves and windows. I thought that withdrawal was finally over. This was a very brief window and the symptoms soon returned. The early part of the post-acute period was profoundly challenging. When I reviewed the journal entries, I could see how much they reflect the thick brain fog and incoherence I was experiencing at that time. Although most are disjointed and uninspiring, I hope they will give further insight into the dynamics of the recovery process.

JOURNAL LOGS

February 26, 2006

MY FIRST WINDOW

Today the veil has been gently lifted and everything is bright and glowing. The sun is emerging after what seems like years in another universe. I am filled with hope and a knowing that withdrawal has at last ended. I feel like a new person.

This is overwhelming. I cannot recall being this lucid since the late 1990s. It feels great to be able to feel again, to connect with myself and others, and to have energy to do the little things that were impossible to do just a few days ago.

I am so grateful for my healing. It has been a long time but my precious brain has finally readjusted to being without the dreaded pill.

July 8, 2006

PATIENTLY WAITING

It was bad timing. I had my follow up consultation with the neurologist earlier this week and was in the throes of withdrawal. When I saw him at the end of February, the symptoms were less intense. I mentioned withdrawal and he said it does not last this long.

This time I didn't say anything. I was perspiring profusely, my hands were visibly shaking, and I know I looked like I should have been immediately admitted to their psychiatric wing. I could sense his concern as he observed the symptoms. When he asked if

I would be willing to see a neuropsychiatrist, I knew there was no way I could justify declining.

What is going to happen to me if no one believes that this is still withdrawal? I don't know how much longer the symptoms will persist. It has been 11 months since my last dose of clonazepam, and almost seven since my last diazepam. Apart from the usual symptoms, the light and hearing sensitivity is intense. Barely managed to watch Wimbledon and every sound freaks me out. I thought I would have been back at work by now but there is no way I could cope with even a part-time job. I can't believe how persistent these symptoms are. This is unfathomable. All I can do is wait.

August 29, 2006

RECOVERY ON SCHEDULE

I still cannot tolerate the computer screen for long; I can't focus to read either. It doesn't matter anyway, because with this impaired cognition nothing makes sense. Somehow I can cope with staring mindlessly at the television screen and it is now my new companion. I watch everything and cannot miss the 'Friends', 'Frasier', 'Keeping Up Appearances' and 'Seinfeld' reruns. They make me laugh.

There is nothing I can do but accept that I need to allow whatever my nervous system deems necessary to unfold. This is a great lesson in patience for me. Fighting what is happening won't make it go away. I will keep reminding myself that I am getting better, even if at times it doesn't appear to be so. My recovery is right on schedule.

September 9, 2006

HAPPY BIRTHDAY, DEAR MOTHER

The path of least resistance is ahead of me. It is the only one I can take while I observe my nervous system in overdrive and shake my head in disbelief. Today would have been my mother's birthday. I miss her. If she were here she would have put her arms around me and said, 'Darling, this too, shall pass'. Yes, Mum, I know my healing is taking place. This is why the symptoms are present. You are right, this will pass.

December 20, 2006

QUIET CHRISTMAS

It has been a long year. I am starting to have a few more windows and have accepted that my recovery is on schedule. I have been benzo-free for a year and although it has been a challenging one, I have no regrets. I know I'm going to be okay. This will be a quiet Christmas. I'm going to be alone but of my own volition. Coping with gatherings and other festive events is too much for me at this time. My friends and family understand my need to be on my own. I have been fortunate in this regard. A few days ago I had a little window but another wave is here. The fog is too thick for me to write more.

March 29, 2007

A SPRING WINDOW

The long wave has ended and I am enjoying another window. I love these windows because they give reassuring glimpses of recovery. I have stopped anticipating waves or windows. It has taken me this long to learn about relinquishing control. True power lies in totally surrendering.

Now I tell myself that if another wave comes it is because it is meant to, and if this window lasts indefinitely it is also because it is meant to. I can't control the recovery process. I can only accept that whatever emerges is a necessary part of my healing.

Today, I shall enjoy this window. I won't worry about resurgence of symptoms or anything else. Spring is here. I will sit in the garden and watch the swans and ducks glide by. This is a good day. I am grateful for my healing.

June 1, 2007

ANOTHER WAVE

The past few nights have been weird. I guess I'm having another wave of residual symptoms as I'm unable to sleep for more than 20 minutes at a time because the involuntary muscle movements keep waking me up. I've tried chamomile tea and drops of lavender on my pillow. They don't seem to be helping and could even be making things worse. I'm doing all the right things, I think: comfortable temperature, dark room, no television or other stimulation, but to no avail.

I am tired. I know this will pass so I won't get too stressed. When I can't sleep I do my diaphragmatic breathing and repeat a few affirmations. Then I doze off again until another spasm wakes me up.

Despite everything, I am still grateful that I don't have the numerous symptoms that I had a year ago. I am grateful for my healing. *All is well. I am well.*

June 5, 2007

WALKING THE TALK

This recent wave of withdrawal has certainly been a test for me. It has been a challenge for me to follow my own advice. So often I've written about being patient and gentle with oneself yet I've spent the last few hours disturbed by the resurfacing of the distended abdomen, dizziness and other symptoms. It has been the most intense wave within the past six months.

I was looking forward to resuming my normal activities. The resurgence of these symptoms means I have had to cut down on the exercise routines I started when the last period of clarity began. I've also had to make other lifestyle adjustments such as eliminating wheat from my diet because of the benzo belly.

What can I say? I have a choice. I can remind myself that this angst will only contribute to my discomfort and refocus. I will think of how much better I am than a few months ago, of how fortunate I am to be over the worst. I will affirm my wellness with the knowing that I have already received my healing. I will see all the good in my life now and that good will expand. I am grateful for my healing. *I am well. All is well.*

June 26, 2007

CHALLENGING WAVE

The current wave of withdrawal is finally receding. It started with the distended abdomen, progressed to severe dizziness, and profuse sweating and ended up with me spending the last ten days under my duvet with chills, sweats, tooth and gum pain, brain fog, joint/muscle pain and almost constant spasming.

This wave lasted a full month. It was the longest since December's. I am shocked that the symptoms could be so intense this long after discontinuing the drug. Such is the nature of withdrawal. This is a true example of the uniqueness of each person's experience. There is just no rhyme or reason, no pattern, and nothing makes sense.

It gets better though and eventually the waves will decrease in frequency until they stop recurring. For now, I am looking forward to enjoying this window of clarity with the hope that it will remain open indefinitely. Who knows? I am patient with myself and all is well. *This too, shall pass.*

July 19, 2007

THE LONG ROAD TURNS

Today has been another good day. One of the good things about this experience is my new ability to take each day as it comes, to be patient and to go with the flow. I used to be a go-getter, 'monitor the process and ensure the result' kind of person. Now I can let go and trust that the outcome will be for my highest good without knowing how or when.

When I had my last wave of withdrawal, I reminded myself of the fact that when we set out on a long journey by car along an unfamiliar winding road, we can only see a few hundred yards ahead at a time. Yet we trust that we will get to our destination and more often than not, we do.

Sometimes, when it seems that this withdrawal journey will never end and frustration, desolation and anxiety threaten to take over, trust that you are on the right track. You will reach your 'fully recovered drug-free' destination when the timing is right. Even the longest road has a turning.

This window lasted a week and was followed by another long period of more unrelenting symptoms which abated briefly in late August. By this time I had become truly accepting of the process. I knew I could not predict whether a wave or another window was on its way. I had come to accept that withdrawal was definitely my life lesson in patience, acceptance and total surrender.

September 2, 2007

I AM WELL

Today has been one of those days. I've been having a few withdrawal reminders but nothing to make me think another wave is approaching. I have not had the classic profuse sweating or mouth/teeth pain so I'd be surprised if what I'm experiencing lasts longer than a few days.

My current symptoms include joint stiffness and muscle pain, especially those in my back. So I'm taking my own advice and having some 'self-nurturing bordering on totally indulgent' time-out.

I know I will be fine soon. As I always remind myself, this is nothing compared to even six months ago. I will continue to give thanks for my healing. *I am well. All is well.*

September 5, 2007

BENZO BELLY AND MORE

More withdrawal symptoms have surfaced over the past few days. The benzo belly is back and I look as if I'm about to give birth. My body feels very, very heavy. A slow walk up the stairs is leaving me breathless and tired. I literally flop on the bed where I have to rest for a while before attempting to move again. I've also been having chills, sweats, dizziness and the nausea is back. The spaciness, brain fog and other head stuff have also resurfaced.

What can I do? Often, when a wave of withdrawal returns, I am tempted to question whether or not something else is wrong. If I did not have my windows, I know I would be even more doubtful. But I am glad I have not had the dreaded mouth and teeth pain. I am dealing with the other symptoms by resting, eating sensibly, listening to soothing music and being patient.

This morning I reminded myself that this is just another wave which will soon pass. Nothing I say or do will accelerate my recovery and the more agitated and impatient I become, the less likely it is that I will feel well, even if only emotionally. *This too, shall pass.* I am grateful for my healing and all is well.

September 22, 2007

OUR ESSENCE

'We are never given more than we can handle.' This cliché came to mind today and although it is often overused, it is true. The mere fact that we are still here, still hopeful and healing (which we are even if it seems like it is taking forever) is confirmation of this. Then I thought, to be 'given' dependency and withdrawal must mean that we are inherently strong enough both emotionally and physically, and courageous beyond measure. No matter how shaky, fragile and traumatized we may be feeling as we go through withdrawal or its aftermath, we must remember this and acknowledge this part of ourselves that we can never lose.

At the core of our being is our essence. This has remained unchanged and unharmed from the drug and will once again become evident. It is who we really are and to over-identify with our symptoms means we could end up forgetting our true selves. It is good for those of us going through withdrawal to spend time reminding ourselves of our core qualities, the ones that may not always be apparent during withdrawal but which we know are still there, and always will be.

September 26, 2007

HOPE

'Hope is a good thing, maybe the best of things, and no good thing ever dies' is a quote from one of my all-time favourite movies, Stephen King's 'The Shawshank Redemption'. It is so easy to lose hope when a situation takes longer than anticipated to be resolved, or when our egos interfere in our healing by trying to control the process, as in how and when. The key then, I tell myself, is to let go and not have a timeline or other expectation. I can use what I have now, today, to be comfortable and make my life as pleasant as possible.

This was my gentle reminder this morning after waking up feeling spaced out and with other benzo reminders which I am choosing to ignore. Instead, I am about to curl up on my sofa and watch 'The Shawshank Redemption' for the umpteenth time. Today is a good day.

October 4, 2007

NON-RESISTANCE

I am now being reminded of how remarkable our bodies are as I can literally feel the recovery process taking place. It seems as if the tooth and mouth pain is gone for good. It did not resurface during the last two withdrawal waves and has been replaced with a constant tinnitus and intensified dizziness. I am beginning to get that sense of my entire central nervous system being readjusted and retuned.

Along with the tinnitus and dizziness I am having other symptoms but I won't give them much energy. Instead I am honouring my loyal body for coping with these new 'surprises' as well as the unrelenting ones.

For those of us in protracted withdrawal, making a conscious choice to not resist the symptoms and to accept them as being a part of the healing process really helps. At least it does for me and I hope it will for you too. As I write this my head is spinning but there is this voice inside saying, 'It's okay, just be grateful for your healing'.

October 8, 2007

HEALING REFLECTION

Always know that no matter what you are going through, at your deepest level the essence of who you are still exists. Irrespective of the drug's effects that have resulted in temporary challenges, you remain that special person who entered this world as a beautiful, healthy baby. Even if recovery is seeming to take a long time, always remember that your situation is temporary.

Know that despite your symptoms, your body is restoring itself to its natural state of good health and wellness, even while you are reading now. These recent experiences will only strengthen you and teach you valuable life lessons.

No matter what your symptoms are or what your life is like at present, when you are healed you will resume a fully functional role as parent, spouse, friend and most of all, a strong, resilient you. No one can take your place – that assigned space that only you in your own special way with your unique experiences can fill. Although you are currently facing these challenges, the special purpose that you came here to fulfil is unfolding.

Remember this during any times of doubt – how good it is to still be here and what a precious gift you are. Take time to see that every day, in many ways, you are fortunate. Gently let go of any concerns about whether or not you will heal and choose to find peace in your situation as it is now, today.

Take a deep breath, exhale, and relax into that warm, tender feeling of knowing that all is well and that your recovery is taking place. *This too, shall pass.*

October 23, 2007

SHELL-SHOCKED

Today has been a funny one. I don't know why, but I feel shell-shocked. Occasionally I become overwhelmed with this bizarre issue. I think because I have not had a good window of clarity recently to replenish my emotional reserves, I feel a bit numb.

I know this hiatus won't last long. I now understand the concerns of some of my friends here who have not yet had any windows. To go for such a long period with depersonalization, derealization and other psychological and physical symptoms must be daunting. If I, who have had quite a few windows, am finding this prolonged wave to be so challenging, I can't begin to imagine how they must feel.

Anyway, this is when we have to remain hopeful and also make the best of now. I keep reminding myself of all the encouraging stories I have heard of people who resumed normality post-recovery. The darkest hour is just before dawn. December 17 will be two years since I completed my full taper. Many people find that during the third year the nervous system begins to settle down and the receptors complete their up-regulation process. In the meantime, while I wait, I will make the best of today knowing that every symptom I experience is evidence of the healing that is taking place. I am grateful for my healing.

November 12, 2007

FEELING BETTER

Soon I will be two years completely benzo-free and, oh, how much better I feel compared to this time last year! I can only encourage anyone who is still experiencing withdrawal to try to let go of anxieties about your recovery. It is taking place now, even while you are reading this. At this very moment, bad symptoms or not, windows or not, you are getting better. Your nervous system is recovering and you are healing. The windows will begin to appear, then they will keep getting bigger, brighter and clearer until one day they become an open door ushering you into a world of mental, emotional and physical good health and wellness.

November 16, 2007

YET ANOTHER WAVE

Today is an 'under the blanket' day. Somehow, the symptoms are back, especially the spaced out feeling and dizziness. I feel so strange. Everything seems dull and dark. I feel heavy, exhausted and lethargic, although I've done nothing. Really, how much longer can this go on?

I'm not feeling sorry for myself, just petulant. This is when I have to remind myself to be patient and trust that the healing is taking place, even though it may not feel that way. Ah well, such is the nature of withdrawal. All I can do is say more affirmations, nurture myself and wait. *This too, shall pass.*

November 30, 2007

ANOTHER WINDOW

I am experiencing another beautiful window and it is reassuring. Am beginning to get a clearer picture of what recovery will be like. To elaborate, for those who have not yet tapered or experienced windows of clarity: It is like getting lost in a fog for a long, long period, then going through a tunnel and emerging to find yourself in a beautiful garden. The flowers are bright, the sun is shining, skies are clear blue, and birds are singing; emotions you had forgotten existed are threatening to overwhelm.

I had a meeting midweek and was pleased that I was coherent and lucid enough to concentrate. Now, with the abating of many of the symptoms, I am better able to assess what life post-benzos may bring. I know I am not totally symptom-free as the distorted hearing, muscle spasms and a few others are still present. However, compared to how I felt during the recent unpleasant wave of symptoms, this is pure bliss.

The best thing about having a window, apart from feeling much improved, is that it contradicts what the well-meaning doctors and other doubters have said. If what we are experiencing is not withdrawal related, why is there a pattern? Why do most of the symptoms completely disappear at the same time? And why did they appear at the time of tapering off the drug? I am grateful for these windows; they keep me hopeful.

PROGRESS REPORTS

If you are frustrated because you anticipated a much quicker recovery, you could benefit from doing a progress report or what could be referred to as a little comparison exercise. Whenever I felt discouraged or concerned about the symptoms persisting for too long, or subsiding only to return in waves, I would remind myself of my pre-taper and acute withdrawal days.

Then I would think of my progress during the post-acute withdrawal months. It never failed to put my recovery into perspective. I would think of how spaced out, how lethargic, zombie-like and unfocused I was, along with the host of other issues that made me go online to find out what was wrong with me in the first place. This would make me appreciate my decision to discontinue the drug, with absolutely no regrets.

I would then think about the unpleasant acute withdrawal months and that was enough to lift my energy. Acknowledging that the vomiting, weird perception distortion and other psychological symptoms were gone was all I needed to do to appreciate the progress I had made.

Then I would think back to the previous three or six months. I would be pleasantly surprised that some of the symptoms were no longer present. I remember feeling thankful that I was so much better. I would congratulate myself for coping and for making it through the worst part of withdrawal.

Finally, I would reassure myself that if I survived those months and had made such significant progress, then I could only imagine how well I would feel in another six months.

If in your case you haven't seen any progress, don't let this discourage you. Recovery is not linear and sometimes symptoms intensify or new ones appear before there is any evidence of healing. And not everyone has windows. Some people go for a long time with no improvements only to find that later on, within weeks sometimes, most or all of the symptoms disappear, never to return. Whatever your pattern turns out to be, you must remain optimistic and continue to remind yourself that the natural outcome of withdrawal is recovery.

Sometimes there is an inclination to get immersed in thoughts of doubt, which in turn causes us to forget that the symptoms are going to eventually go away. This preoccupation makes us focus intently on everything that is going wrong and it can test our patience and fortitude, making us scared and desperate.

These thoughts are fuelled by fear and this is when it is necessary to remind yourself that withdrawal is temporary, that every symptom you experience is present because you have discontinued the drug. Your receptors must be repaired in order for you to recover.

If you acknowledge a symptom as a necessary part of your recovery – evidence that it is taking place – you may end up feeling less resistant. You will then be able to accept that you are weeks or months away from being well again. You will know that you are in the process of regaining control of your life. This was the reason you decided to discontinue the drug in the first place. I recall wondering if my protracted withdrawal would ever end. Today, I can hardly remember what it was like. Trust that it will be the same for you.

8 COPING TOOLS

One of the most successful strategies for coping with withdrawal is to make the decision prior to or early in the tapering process to accept the symptoms without resisting and to use techniques found to be most effective for self-management. Attitude can make a significant, positive difference during withdrawal. I have seen people with very high anxiety and numerous physical and psychological symptoms cope better than others with very few symptoms and reportedly lower anxiety levels. This is because they are non-resistant and use as many tools as possible to manage their symptoms.

Quite often the withdrawal-induced combination of dark, depressive moods and anxiety results in an inability to feel motivated. One may become void of energy and unable to initiate positive self-talk or any other anxiety-reducing approach. When this is the case, the use of external aids, such as relaxation CDs, regular grounding and breathing exercises, can elicit favourable results.

There are, however, a few important factors to be considered. Depending on how severe withdrawal is, it can be challenging to focus long enough to learn something new, especially if cognition is affected. Also, some people are emotionally and mentally fragile and report feeling raw, exposed and vulnerable; they may find some techniques to be too emotive. In such cases, caution should be exercised and only the simplest and most appropriate ones should be attempted.

Emotional safety is key at this time. If you live alone and are unsupported, or if you are experiencing intense depersonalization, derealization, adrenaline surges, feelings of impending doom, distorted auditory, visual or tactile perception, organic fear or other psychological withdrawal symptoms, you may want to try a simple practice instead. You could try focusing on your breath or talking yourself through the symptoms. If you plan on attempting a new technique which requires a consultation, please ensure that the practitioner is licensed and qualified and that you have safe and adequate support.

The following tools (presented in alphabetical order) can be used to cope during withdrawal. They help with anxiety and stress-related issues. Some are also good techniques that can be used post-recovery especially in cases where anxiety was a pre-existing condition. Not all of these will resonate or be suited to you, but through trial and error you will find a few safe, reliable methods which will help you to manage your symptoms.

AFFIRMATIONS AND POSITIVE SELF-TALK

Speaking positively to yourself or using affirmations is a most powerful coping tool which can be used during withdrawal. It is a cognitive behavioural therapy (CBT) technique which has been proven to be successful in the treatment of anxiety and depression. How you speak to yourself and the thoughts you focus on can strongly influence your mood and how well you cope. Being aware of your inner dialogue and gently changing a negative thought to a constructive and positive counter-thought is a good way of remaining optimistic.

I first started using affirmations after reading *You Can Heal Your Life* by Louise Hay many years ago. The use of positive self-talk when working with clients presenting with anxiety and depression was included in the CBT modules of my university's post-graduate counselling training. Contrary to what some believe, there is nothing 'new-agey' or mysterious about them. Everyone uses affirmations and positive or negative self-talk daily, whether we acknowledge that we do or not. A thought of concern is as much an affirmation as any of the positive statements. Repeatedly saying or thinking, 'This symptom just won't go away' or 'My withdrawal is not ending' are classic examples.

If nothing else, on a cognitive level, affirmations drown the worry thoughts and make room for more positive ones that contribute to emotional well-being. Even if you are unable to connect with your feelings because of emotional bluntness, instead of the energy going to thoughts of fear and dread, the focus will be on your healing and you will benefit.

By the time you've repeated a few affirmations, you will notice an energy shift and the fear will be replaced by a more hopeful feeling. Despite the symptoms being present, you will be responding differently. This is because you are now in alignment with how you want to feel rather than being overwhelmed by how you do not want to feel. It is powerful.

It is okay if a positive affirmation sounds feeble and unconvincing in the beginning. Your resistance is understandable and the idea is not to struggle against your authentic experience. However, it is still worth exploring. You may be pleasantly surprised, and not with negative side effects. You will find that in spite of how you may be feeling, if you continue saying a positive statement, you will gradually get to the point where you begin to believe that it is possible for you to get better. This is how affirmations work.

Try to get into the habit of noticing your thought patterns – not obsessively – just gently being aware of the worrying, anxious ones. (This works for withdrawal-induced thoughts as well.) Once you identify thoughts straying towards the symptoms, concerns or other fears, you can gently acknowledge them and, without judgement, say something such as: 'It's okay that I'm having these thoughts. It is normal for me to think this way. I also know that my recovery is taking place and that every day, in some way, I am getting better.'

There is nothing to lose by doing this. You can say affirmations periodically throughout the day – whatever feels right for you and as often as you like – the more frequently, the better. You can say them in front of the mirror or write them down; if you have a journal or notebook and feel up to writing, you can allow yourself to get carried away. The key to getting the best effect is saying them with emotion, conviction and resolve. In addition, visualizing yourself fully recovered and imagining what it will feel like will create a more powerful shift in energy.

It is best to stick to one or two affirmations and not do too many at once; keep it simple. Less will produce more focus and the more often you repeat one statement, the easier it will be for it to begin to ring true. It works; you do not need anyone's approval or to justify or scientifically prove this. All you need to do is experiment and see what happens. Affirm only what you want and don't mention the symptoms; the focus is on wellness. Here are a few to get you started (you can also make up your own):

'My body is self-healing and restores itself to perfect health.'

'Every day, in every way, I am getting better and better.'

'My mind is sound and my body is healthy.'

'Wellness is my natural state of being.'

'I am healthy in spirit, mind and body.'

If using 'I am' statements is too unrealistic for you, you can try saying 'I can be' or 'I will be' statements instead. For example, 'My body is self-healing and will restore itself to good health.' Sometimes it can be challenging to believe that such a simple technique is so powerful. The mind is indeed powerful and it is good that we can change our thoughts.

BREATHING

Even if nothing else works for you, finding a good breathing technique will have a positive influence and help to calm your nervous system. It is one of the most natural tranquillisers. You can mindfully practise a breathing technique: The simplest way to start is by letting your mind gently focus on your breath as you take air in and out slowly. You will begin to create a rhythm as you become more aware of your breathing pattern and it becomes steadier.

You can inhale to the count of 1-2-3 and then slowly exhale through the mouth to the count of 1-2-3-4. You can increase the counts as you find your rhythm and it begins to feel unforced. There are other variations which work well too and will help to calm you, including the 4-7-8 exercise where you inhale quietly through your nostrils to the count of 1-2-3-4, hold for 7 counts then exhale through your mouth, pursing your lips, to the count of 8. Try to keep the tip of your tongue behind your upper front teeth while doing this 4-7-8 exercise. When you first begin, do no more than four repetitions at a time and then gradually increase with practice.

DIAPHRAGMATIC BREATHING

Diaphragmatic breathing is useful in the treatment of anxiety and hyperventilation. It involves breathing deeply into your lungs by flexing your diaphragm. When we breathe diaphragmatically, our stomach and abdomen expand rather than the chest. Here is a modified version which, if used properly, will help you to relax. I found it to be especially useful when I was having sleep difficulty.

Lie on your back with knees bent and put your hand just below your rib cage. Then breathe in slowly, focusing on the breath and the feel of your hand as your stomach moves (out when inhaling and in when exhaling).

This can be done initially for 5–10 minutes about four times daily. It is also useful for whenever you feel anxious, have difficulty sleeping or feel a panic attack coming on. It can also be done sitting in a comfortable position. It is safe to gradually increase the time you spend doing it. Try to have a longer out-breath than in-breath. You can also breathe out with pursed lips through your mouth.

EMOTIONAL FREEDOM TECHNIQUE

Emotional freedom technique (EFT) is an acupressure technique often described as psychological acupuncture. It is easy to learn and effective in the treatment of many conditions. They are widely recognized as a coping tool for anxiety-related issues and are found to be useful during withdrawal.

EFT involves tapping with the fingertips on special meridian points on the face, body and hands while repeating statements designed to provide release from the negative emotions. It is not necessary to understand how EFT works in order to benefit from it.

There are different variations of the technique, but when I was challenged with serious withdrawal symptoms and found it hard to focus, I did a mini version which was still effective. (More information on EFT can be found in the Resources Guide at the back of this book.) You will also find very good EFT videos on the Internet.

EXERCISE

Exercise is beneficial and conducive to wellness. If you are able to do any form of exercise during withdrawal you will fare better. If you have not had a regular exercise regimen and have decided to implement a routine to help you through withdrawal, please do so gradually and at a gentle pace, as too vigorous exercise too quickly can over-stimulate the nervous system and exacerbate symptoms.

Even aerobic exercise, which is known to be beneficial in reducing anxiety and depression, can trigger adrenaline rushes that may worsen withdrawal symptoms. If you are finding that you react sensitively to stimuli, low-impact exercise, such as simple yoga postures or *asanas*, light swimming, stretching or walking outdoors are other safe options.

It is sometimes difficult to identify triggers because of the complexities of withdrawal and the many confounding factors. If you do notice a flare-up of symptoms, extreme lethargy or fatigue after commencing a new exercise regimen, it could mean that the additional stimulation is more than your nervous system can cope with at this time. Sticking to less strenuous exercise may then be your only option. Our bodies are brilliant at communicating and will always guide us. All we need to do is listen.

FAITH

The healing power of faith has long been discussed and studied, and still remains controversial. The medical profession acknowledges that people who profess a faith in a higher power generally are better able to deal with illness, and Twelve-Step groups recognize such faith as a cornerstone of recovery. Conversely, to tell those who hold no particular belief to have faith will likely yield no results.

Quite often we receive calls and emails from those who believe they would not have survived the depths of withdrawal without their faith. This is what has kept them sane, comforted and optimistic. Others have shared that the impact and intensity of withdrawal sent them straight back to the faith of their childhood or in search of spiritual sustenance.

One important aspect of faith which can be beneficial during withdrawal involves the use of prayer to acquire a deeply tranquil state. Repetitive prayer can produce a similar effect to the use of a mantra, or prayer words can be used in place of a mantra to reach a deep state of meditation. The use of prayer beads can also induce a meditative effect. The Roman Catholic rosary, the Hindu *japa mala*, Buddhist *juzu* or Muslim *mishbaha* have all been used in combination with repetitive prayer, with very positive effects. (Even if you have no particular faith, listening to, chanting or singing a mantra like the Tibetan *Om Mani Padme Hum* or the Nichiren Buddhist *Nam Myoho Renge Kyo* can be very soothing.)

The belief in and use of prayer is a very effective tool in providing hope and consolation during withdrawal. In addition, some people receive support from their faith-based groups and churches as they struggle to cope. If you believe in God, Source, Spirit, Buddha, Allah, Krishna – whatever your concept of a supreme force – you will be able to appreciate and relate to the power of faith. You may have found that it has helped you to cope better with your withdrawal. Faith is a lifeline for many.

GROUNDING

These are good, effective techniques which can be used to help you to feel grounded and more connected. They are particularly useful if you are experiencing feelings of anxiety, depersonalization or derealization:

- Feel your feet on the floor (take your shoes off if appropriate), and become aware of your bottom on the chair. Mentally note the sensation, the weight and the connection, and stay with it for a while.

- Look around you. Notice the colour of the wall, are there any paintings, any plants in the room? If there is a clock, notice the time and then remind yourself of what day of the week it is and the date.

- Focus on your breathing and take deep, slow breaths – in through your nose and out through your mouth.

- If you are outside, bring yourself to the present by becoming aware of the feel of the sun on your skin, or the rain if it's raining. If you can, lean against a tree.

Inhale the scents of the grass and other plants. Listen to the sounds around you.

- Keep at least three items of different textures – something soft such as a stuffed toy, something smooth, rubbery, rough, etc. As you hold them let the feel register and connect with them through your sense of touch.

- Imagine that your feet have roots that sink into the ground/ earth. As you stand or sit, feel your feet making contact with the earth and deeply tune in to the connection. If appropriate and you are able to take your shoes off when you do this, it is even better.

- Stroke your cat or dog while being mindful. Say what you are doing while you do it. ('I am stroking my cat.') Your pet may think your actions are strange, but who else is capable of such unconditional acceptance?

HOBBIES

Coping with an intense withdrawal often uses up all one's emotional resources. It can be all-consuming and may impact every area of life. In the early, acute stage, every fibre of your being may be in survival mode leaving very little energy to tend to other issues, and this is understandable. However, it is important to begin to rebalance as soon as your receptors permit. This will prevent stagnation and will keep you from falling into any kind of rut. So as soon as you can, start doing whatever is possible to recreate a balanced life.

At the same time, it is important to be cautious and to pace yourself in order to avoid over-stimulation or setbacks. Getting the balance right is always a work in progress: you set small goals while still being gentle and self-nurturing. Pursuing a hobby is a good place to start. It can be as simple as watercolour painting, journaling (about something other than withdrawal), playing an instrument, knitting or anything that appeals which isn't too stimulating. You could get a pet if you are well enough to take care of it. Cats and dogs are excellent companions, but if you feel that will be too demanding for you, you could get a goldfish, bird or hamster.

Then, in time, you begin to add other activities. You could choose ones that involve others and will help you to reintegrate. This is very important. Some people stay stuck – they eat, breathe and sleep withdrawal long after recovery because no effort was ever made to get the balance right. Think about it and see what you can do.

JIN SHIN JYUTSU

Jin Shin Jyutsu is a simple style of acupressure which has a powerful, soothing effect. It is a non-invasive, ancient Japanese approach to healing. Since discovering its naturally tranquillizing potential, I have recommended it to many in withdrawal and the feedback has been so positive, I thought I would share it with you here.

Jin Shin Jyutsu is very simple to do. It involves using one hand to hold the thumb or finger of the other. Each digit represents a different emotion. The thumb relates to worry, the index finger to fear, the middle finger to anger, the ring finger to sadness/ grief and the little finger to pretense.

This Thumb Hold, as shown above, is very effective for dealing with sleep difficulty. All you need to do is gently wrap one hand around your thumb and hold it for at least 2 minutes. Hold it for as long as you want. You can also switch hands. There are no rules. Some people sleep holding their thumb all night. The favourite hold for our withdrawal friends with intense anxiety is the Index Finger Hold. To do this, gently wrap one hand around the index finger of the other and hold it for as long as you like. You can do this with any finger. There is much more to Jin Shin Jyutsu, so if you are interested please check the Internet. The different ways of holding the fingers result in varying influences on the body, but they are all effective. If you do try it, I hope it will prove to be useful.

MEDITATION

Meditating is another good way of coping with a withdrawal-influenced, compromised nervous system. Being able to learn a formal method of meditation can be challenging for those in intense withdrawal. They may not be able to sit up or maintain postures for prolonged periods due to the somatic effects such as agitation, extreme dizziness, muscle pain, shaking and involuntary movements; or they may be having obsessive, repetitive thoughts and are unable to focus. But for those with tolerable symptoms, meditation can be used to derive welcome periods of restfulness.

When practising meditation, the attention is usually focused on either the breath, a sound, a mantra or imagery. Here is a simple technique:

- Sit up in a comfortable position.

- Close your eyes.

- Breathe in and out through your nose.

- Concentrate on your breath noticing the air going in and air coming out.

- If your mind wanders, gently bring it back to the breath.

It is that simple. You can do this for 5 minutes initially, gradually increasing the time as you become more comfortable with the practice. This can be expanded with the introduction of visualization of a calming scene.

MINDFULNESS

Mindfulness is being in touch with the present moment. You intentionally observe and become aware of your subjective experience – your thoughts, sensations and feelings – without judgement or resistance. You can be mindful when eating, breathing, thinking, hearing, sitting, walking and in many other ways.

By sensing your breath, your body and your immediate environment, you remain fully present and aware, and mental distractions are not resisted or judged. Mindfulness is an excellent skill to practise when coping with withdrawal – a time when you may be prone to worrying thoughts about symptoms and recovery. It can be used to take a step back from your situation and to reduce the impact that withdrawal may be having on your life. It is also a valuable tool to use in everyday life.

The following simple exercise will give you an idea of how mindfulness works. It is not used to stop the mind but it will help you to gently release any thoughts of the past or future and redirect your attention to the present moment by focusing on the breath:

- Find a comfortable position and close your eyes.

- Focus your attention on your breathing. Simply pay attention first to the sensation of your breath as it flows in and out of your nostrils.

- Feel your abdomen rise and fall as you breathe in and out (rising when you inhale and falling as you slowly release the breath).

- Continue to focus your attention on the flow and rhythm of your body as you breathe in and out.

- If thoughts enter your mind (as they probably will), gently acknowledge them as you would clouds passing by and return your focus to your breath.

Do this for as long as you feel comfortable – for as long as it feels right for you. The more you practise, the more natural it will feel and the longer you will be able to do it. You can further extend this basic exercise by moving your attention to the body as you breathe. Place your awareness on one area at a time and notice the sensations. Does it feel cold, warm, tight, sore, tingling? Simply observe, again, without judgement. Just be present. Then when it feels right for you, prepare yourself to open your eyes and slowly do so. You can then ground yourself by doing as follows:

- Slowly open your eyes and look around as if you are seeing for the first time.

- Settle your eyes on an object for about 15–30 seconds. Don't analyse or evaluate it; just observe it.

- As you do this, maintain an awareness of your breathing, your body and any sounds around you.

- Let your eyes rest on another object for a minute or two, until you are ready to get up.

If there is one technique that will be useful for everyone post-recovery, especially if there were problems with anxiety, insomnia or any psychological issue, it is mindfulness. Try it and see.

'SUNSHINE' BOX

Making a 'sunshine' box to brighten the very dark, cloudy days is another tool that helps. Find an attractive box and fill it with uplifting items: You could print off your favourite success stories, get your best inspirational quotes, and make a gratitude list or write affirmations on cards using brightly coloured pens. You also could add a DVD of your favourite funny movie, photos and cards that bring happy memories and make you feel good, other memorabilia of happy times, one or two of your favourite books, loving letters you've received, and clippings of jokes and funny stories that you've found either online, in magazines or in newspapers. You could even write reassuring notes telling yourself you are going to make it to recovery and everything is going to be okay. Anything that lifts your mood is permitted; it may take a packet of almonds or your favourite healthy snack to make you smile. Then, on the days when you feel overwhelmed and can't imagine that the sun could possibly be shining behind the clouds, you get your 'sunshine' box out. (Some people use a folder instead of a box.) You can curl up on the sofa with these gems that help you to forget your troubles, and enjoy indulging all the senses.

Whatever your choice, the idea is to keep this mood enhancer close at hand. It can take time to complete the box but you can do it gradually, at the times when you are best able to focus. Then have it on standby for the days when you feel the worst – the days when you need to make your own sunshine.

SUPPORT GROUPS

I vaguely recall joining a forum sometime in late 2003 or early 2004. I was so spaced out I don't remember exactly when, which forum or what my user name was. After registering I never logged on because I could not relate to what I was reading. I think I read one or two posts and thought there was no way such misery could be my demise. I had no real understanding of withdrawal issues and the challenges people genuinely encounter. It was not until my second year of withdrawal that I wisely joined several forums, and although I only logged on a few times to connect with others in protracted withdrawal, I got some much-needed support and validation.

I remember the suggestion once being made that the Internet support for withdrawal is just mass hysteria and melodrama from people trying to sue their doctors or 'big pharma'. On the contrary, without these online groups, the thousands of people who have no other support – whose families and doctors have limited knowledge of tapering or withdrawal syndrome – would not cope well. In addition, these Internet groups are where those in protracted withdrawal – who are at risk of being misdiagnosed – find reassurance. They are fortunate to have this guidance and additional support when most needed.

It is also true that there are a lot of extremely worried, emotionally fragile, seemingly histrionic, mentally and physically traumatized people in 'withdrawal hell' who understandably post frantic messages. When they relate what they are experiencing this can have an impact on other members. There is no way of avoiding this, as it is rare to find someone who has had a three-week, mildly unpleasant withdrawal joining a group. This is why much of what is read can be disheartening.

If you are distraught and feel vulnerable, take regular breaks from the Internet and distract yourself with positive activities. When you do log on, try not to go through every single post absorbing other members' fear and anxiety related to symptoms you don't even have. Remember, too, that the Internet is accessible to everyone and that there are people in withdrawal who may have other serious mental health issues. Not everything you read will be credible. Also, you will have withdrawal buddies who are so confused and memory impaired that they may make claims of being off one drug but forget to mention they are still tapering off another. When you read a post stating, 'I'm still in withdrawal after five years off' or similar, there is usually more to the story. Don't panic.

If you read something that has an uplifting effect and makes you feel hopeful, bookmark it and keep going back to it or print it. Try not to focus on the symptoms and unfortunate accounts. Supporting other members can also be rewarding, leaving you less preoccupied with your own challenges. Act responsibly when you post and do your best to not frighten those in the earlier stages of withdrawal.

Absorbing everything that can go wrong during withdrawal can make the process seem more daunting than it actually is. When you focus on positive messages that give useful coping tips, the quotes, music, books and movies that are considered to be encouraging, your withdrawal will be more tolerable. You may find that you end up having many good, light, pleasant days despite having to endure the symptoms. The most important things during withdrawal are to look after yourself well and to be emotionally safe.

UNCONSCIOUS MIND EXERCISE

This exercise originated from the teachings of Dr Milton Erickson, a psychiatrist who described the unconscious mind as 'made up of all your learnings over a lifetime, many of which you have completely forgotten, but which serve you in your automatic functioning' (Zeig 1980, p.173):

> Sit or lie in a relaxed position, take a few deep breaths or do a few rounds of your favourite breathing exercise, then say the following sentence out loud: 'Unconscious mind, I now allow you to do whatever you think is necessary in order for me to feel better'.

This single sentence can be a most powerful, effective coping tool if applied accurately. It is the simplest yet most useful technique I have learned to date, and it would be selfish of me to not share it. My older brother, who is a neuro-linguistic programming practitioner, shared it with me when I was having very severe symptoms. He successfully uses this technique with clients and in his personal life. The first time I used it I was in a state of high anxiety and had intense feelings of impending doom. I phoned him, did as instructed when I hung up and immediately went to sleep. I woke up feeling more relaxed and refreshed than I had in months.

The unconscious or subconscious mind is a powerful healer. It is not external of us, will do us no harm and is the part of our psyche that knows best what we need at any given time. It is there to be accessed whenever we need it.

Falling asleep was my natural reaction to this exercise, maybe because deep, rejuvenating sleep was what I needed at that time. However, the unconscious mind will deliver exactly what we request: whatever is necessary for us to feel better. It is our internal guidance system. You may find that without thinking, you pick up the phone and call someone who ends up giving you just the reassurance you need, or you suddenly gain a new perspective of your withdrawal which leads to full acceptance of the symptoms. I can only liken this exercise to having a total release of conscious control or achieving a form of complete surrender.

VISUALIZATION

Visualization involves focusing on an image of what you want and seeing it as already manifested. Although the imagination is used, visualization is more profound than daydreaming or fantasizing. It is a conscious use of one's will to see, in the mind's eye, desired scenes which can be of an event, a specific behaviour or, in the case of withdrawal, being recovered.

It is done in the first person and present tense. When doing visualization, you can explore with all the senses. As you conjure up the image of yourself being fully recovered in your mind, what are you feeling, hearing, smelling and tasting? How is the scene unfolding?

The idea behind visualization in withdrawal is that by directing and controlling the images in your mind, it can be used as a positive distraction to manage and cope with some symptoms. It is best to do a breathing exercise to relax prior to starting your visualization exercise. Visualizing yourself post-recovery is an excellent way to drift off to sleep or simply pass the time.

WORK ON YOUR THOUGHTS

This is another effective CBT approach. Question any doubtful thoughts you may be having about your recovery. Examine the evidence. This is different to using affirmations or positive self-talk. It is about putting things into perspective in order to avoid or minimize catastrophizing.

For most in withdrawal, the two main culprits are: 'What if I never recover?' and 'What if something else is wrong with me?' We call them the dreaded 'what if' thoughts. They are dangerous and can drive you close to insanity. You must remember that they are only thoughts. You don't have to believe them. They are not true. Take a few moments to assess them, then change your perspective: 'Is this definitely, without uncertainty, going to happen?' The answer is *no*.

Yet, these thoughts which trigger a knee-jerk reaction are the source of worry and additional anxiety. They fuel so much fear that, once entertained, a downward spiral begins leading to a most unfortunate sequence of events, culminating in a devastating (imagined) future. All of this anguish comes from a thought that is not even true. How things may appear to you because of your current symptoms differs from the reality – which is that you will heal.

So, when thoughts of a permanent withdrawal or a dreaded disease creep into your mind, work on them. Ask yourself if they are absolutely true and what evidence you have to prove it. Don't try to explain or justify them. 'Am I certain beyond doubt?' No. 'Is there any possibility of another outcome?' *Yes, there is.* The truth – what will serve you best right now – is that your symptoms are due to withdrawal, and recovery is the normal outcome.

9   STIMULANTS, SUPPLEMENTS AND DIET

One of the gifts of withdrawal is that when it is over many people find that they have acquired invaluable information relevant to every aspect of life, including diet and nutrition. They end up eating wholesome, healthy foods, drinking adequate amounts of water, avoiding harmful additives and consequently feel healthier than they did during their pre-withdrawal days.

It is not that everyone coming off an antidepressant or tranquilliser will find it necessary to monitor food, drink and supplement intake; some simply choose to take preventative measures while others continue as usual. For those of you who are faced with gastrointestinal disturbances such as nausea, reflux, diarrhoea, constipation, stomach cramps, spasms, 'travelling' pain and the infamous 'benzo belly', which causes distension, the following information will help you to cope.

With the gastrointestinal tract being sensitive to stress, it is no surprise that these issues surface. Furthermore, there are receptors in this area. Although the function of these receptors has not yet been determined, it is thought that there is a link between their presence and the gastrointestinal withdrawal symptoms that some experience. Even if you are not having digestion issues, this information will be useful and will improve your overall sense of wellness.

SUPPLEMENTS

There are conflicting reports regarding the taking of supplements during withdrawal. Some people report a noticeable negative reaction and others have found that some supplements seem to help. There are certain deficiencies that should not be ignored. For example, if you are anaemic and it is affecting you and making you weak and breathless, then taking an iron supplement or eating iron-rich foods combined with foods high in vitamin C will help. If a restricted diet results in deficiencies and you are able to take supplements without reacting, any problems caused by the deficiencies may be resolved.

Conversely, if you notice that you are sensitive to stimuli during withdrawal and the deficiency is not causing problems, it is best to be cautious and wait until you are at least over the acute and post-acute phases of withdrawal before taking a supplement that may affect the nervous system. In these cases you could try to get your nutrients from food rather than concentrated sources.

Magnesium, calcium, B vitamins, 5-hydroxytryptophan (HTPs), taurine, melatonin, homeopathic remedies, GABA, valerian, kava – all these supplements may be beneficial in non-withdrawal situations, but they cannot accelerate the repair of the GABA receptors. There is no evidence suggesting that they cause withdrawal-induced symptoms to disappear. If your withdrawal is not problematic, then at best they will supply added nutrients. In terms of affecting the duration of withdrawal, anecdotal reports confirm that they can intensify the process in those who are sensitive. The use of supplements during withdrawal continues to be a highly debatable topic.

Taking supplements was ruled out in my case because I reacted every time. I had to be vigilant even in the later stages of recovery. I was not paranoid and it sometimes took a long time for me to identify the supplement in question as being the culprit. Months after my final wave, I tried transdermal magnesium to see if it would help to ease the residual spasms. I was confident about using supplements and did not anticipate being thrown back into a brief period of full withdrawal. I was horrified when I started having sweats, chills, shaking and intense vertigo. At first I thought, 'Imagine having another wave so long after what I thought was recovery', but soon I realized it was a reaction to the magnesium. I stopped using the magnesium spray and had no further recurrence of symptoms. My experience is not unique. I receive many calls and emails from people who have reacted to supplements, and this is the reason caution is recommended. If we could guarantee that no one would react adversely, we would encourage everyone to take them.

If you are already taking supplements and feel that they are making you feel better, there is no need to stop taking them. No flare-up of symptoms is a good indicator that it is okay to continue. If, however, you are having persistent symptoms, eliminating supplements may help to confirm whether or not they are complicating the withdrawal process and hindering your recovery. A hyper-excitable nervous system does not need additional stimulation. Since withdrawal symptoms are due mainly to the down-regulation of our receptors, recovery is dependent on their repair. As far as I am aware, there is no supplement on the market known to accelerate this process. The most important thing during withdrawal is to feel as well as possible. Our bodies are so innately intelligent that they always find ways of communicating.

ALCOHOL

Alcohol is a central nervous system depressant which acts on subtypes of GABA receptors in the brain. It therefore affects the damaged receptors and interferes with the recovery process. It also causes adverse reactions in those coming off antidepressants. If you are still taking a benzo, the combination can be dangerous. Taking alcohol while on antidepressants can worsen depression. If you have already tapered but are still going through withdrawal, having even half a glass of alcohol is known to intensify symptoms.

Look out for hidden alcohol/ethanol in medicines including herbal tinctures and other preparations. Although this level of alcohol will be minuscule and under normal circumstances would have no effect, with a hypersensitive nervous system do not be surprised if you react. Withdrawal can do strange things to the body. I recall taking a cough mixture more than a year into my withdrawal; one dose caused a drastic reaction. My eyes got that old glassy look, I started having chills, shaking and sweating and looked like I was back in acute withdrawal.

As tempting as it may be, having alcohol during withdrawal is not worth the risk, especially if you are having troubling symptoms. It is advisable to avoid it at this time. The poor GABA receptors are already struggling to function and any interference in the process will be detrimental. Unless you eliminate alcohol from your diet, you won't know if it is affecting your recovery. If you like relaxing with a good glass of wine, this is the perfect time to look forward to your recovery when you may once again be able to indulge.

MEDICATION

There are contradictory reports regarding reactions to medication taken during withdrawal. 'Flu-like' symptoms, gastrointestinal disturbances, back pain, 'travelling' pain (moves around the body), burning pain, joint (arthritic type) and muscle pain are common at this time. Some people are able to take over-the-counter remedies without having adverse reactions; others report no relief or aggravated symptoms. These flare-ups tend to occur after the use of some types of antihistamines, opiate and codeine-containing painkillers, and flu remedies which include even minuscule amounts of alcohol/ethanol or caffeine.

Commonly prescribed antibiotics known as quinolones cause severe adverse reactions and should therefore be avoided. If you are prescribed this class of medication, please ask your doctor to find an alternative. It is good to remember also that herbs also have pharmacological effects, some of which may exacerbate symptoms in susceptible individuals.

The best approach is to be observant. With brain fog and other cognitive problems, it is easy to unknowingly overlook simple precautions. Without becoming overly concerned or expectant, be quietly attentive to what you ingest. For those experiencing persistent and problematic symptoms, it is worth checking the labels and enclosed information leaflets. There is no need to panic if you do react; simply stop taking that remedy and find a safer alternative. If you develop a viral infection or other condition that requires medication, it is better to take the recommended treatment and risk a flare-up of symptoms than suffer unnecessarily.

DIETARY MODIFICATIONS

Food is the one pleasure which some people feel they can explore and savour during withdrawal. Those individuals are able to eat normally. Others find that a simple diet works best for them at this time. Since gastric problems are so common, some make the decision to modify their diets early on in their tapers. For those with food sensitivities, blood sugar fluctuations and other troubling symptoms, nutritional balance is an ongoing quest. Any modifications that will make it easier on the digestive system can be used to one's advantage.

CAFFEINE

Caffeine is a stimulant which, if you are already hyper-excitable and are experiencing sleep difficulty, you may want to avoid or consume very little of and only early in the day. Those who are having a difficult withdrawal are advised to completely omit caffeine. If you are accustomed to having several cups of coffee or tea daily, it is best to gradually reduce your intake rather than suddenly abstain. Remember, too, that decaffeinated beverages also contain a small but notable amount of caffeine.

OTHER CONSIDERATIONS

Fluctuations in blood sugar often occur during withdrawal and some people report an exacerbation in symptoms when they consume sugary foods. Many people who write to us or phone have reported that once they cut out or reduced their sugar intake, their symptoms lessened in intensity. This includes chemical sweeteners and ketchup. If you have a sweet tooth, stevia and yacon syrup are good and safe sugar substitutes. Yacon syrup is a natural, raw, low-calorie sweetener made from the root of the yacon plant. Stevia is another natural sweetener made from the leaf of the stevia plant. They both have negligible effects on blood glucose.

Other reported culprits during withdrawal are monosodium glutamate, chocolates, which contain both caffeine and sugar, and very strong spices. Eliminating wheat is recommended if you become constipated or have other digestion issues, and watch out for processed ready meals which contain chemicals. It is not necessary to drink gallons of water, but drinking adequate amounts is advisable.

Consuming small, frequent meals that contain foods with low glycaemic levels is believed to be of value to those with blood sugar fluctuations. Carbohydrates that break down slowly, releasing glucose gradually into the blood stream, have low glycaemic levels. Highly glycaemic foods exacerbate hyperactivity (which is the last thing someone with bad symptoms needs).

This rough guide should give you an idea of the glycaemic-index levels of some common foods:

- *Fruit.* Apples, blackberries, blueberries, raspberries, cherries, grapefruit, kiwis, strawberries, oranges and pears are low. Bananas, mangoes, pineapples, red grapes, fruit cocktail and papayas are medium. Watermelons and dates are high.

- *Vegetables.* Broccoli, alfalfa, cabbage, cauliflower, cucumber, watercress, spinach, tomatoes and Brussels sprouts are low. Sweetcorn and beetroot are medium. Pumpkin, parsnips and swede are high.

- *Other.* Almonds, Brazil nuts and peanuts are low. With the exception of broad beans, most beans and pulses, including lentils and chickpeas, are low. Fish, shellfish and lean, skinless meats are low. Pastas are low to medium, depending on type. Rice, including brown rice, is medium to high, depending on type. Cornflakes, honey-coated, puffed and other processed cereals are high. Potatoes fried, baked and mashed are high. Doughnuts, muffins, white bread, commercial wheat bread and bagels are high.

GREEN SMOOTHIES

If you are troubled with gastric disturbances and have had to modify your diet as well as abstain from supplements, you may be concerned about nutritional deficiencies. I discovered green smoothies post-recovery and have since told friends in withdrawal. The many good reports of improved energy and other benefits that I have received made me decide to share with you this idea of blending fruit with vegetables. This is not an endorsement of green smoothies as a withdrawal cure, but having a green smoothie or two daily will ensure that you're not missing out on a lot of vital nutrients.

Here are two delicious recipes. Some people use just one banana with half an avocado for creaminess and add stevia or yacon syrup to make them sweeter.

Recipe 1

1–2 mangoes

2–3 handfuls of baby spinach or kale

1 cup water

1 banana

Recipe 2

1–2 oranges

1 banana

4–5 strawberries

½ head romaine lettuce

Please note that raw kale and cabbage should be used with caution by anyone with an underactive thyroid, as they are what is termed 'goitrogenous' and interfere with iodine uptake. Also, because kale has a very high concentration of vitamin K, people on anticoagulants (blood thinners) should consider this property as the drug attempts to lower vitamin K.

Even organic fruit and vegetables should be washed thoroughly, so be sure to give them a thorough wash. In order to get your nutrients, the most important thing is to add at least two large portions of fresh, green leafy vegetables to whatever fruit you choose to use. If you are aware or suspect that you react negatively to a certain fruit or vegetable, please do not add it to your smoothie.

Moderation, being vigilant without becoming paranoid and observing the way our bodies respond to stimuli of any kind are the best approaches during withdrawal.

10 SUPPORTING SOMEONE IN WITHDRAWAL

If you are supporting a family member or friend who is coming off an antidepressant, sleeping pill or other benzo tranquilliser, you may find that the usual approaches are not effective. Withdrawal can cause extremely bizarre behaviour and uncommon physical and psychological reactions. This can be overwhelming, and so you may be feeling unsure about how to proceed. The most important thing you can do is be there, be available and almost constantly give encouragement. Be gentle. Comfort him or her in verbal and non-verbal ways. Holding a hand or a gentle touch of reassurance is good, if appropriate. You can let your loved one know it is okay to cry, be angry or be silent – whatever is needed at the time.

Try to withhold judgement and be as patient as possible. An intense withdrawal can take everyone involved into what may seem to be a whirlwind of drama: uncharacteristic behaviour, financial difficulties, relationship friction and more – beyond the realms of reason. But this disruption is temporary and will go with recovery.

COMPASSION FATIGUE

Compassion fatigue or burnout occurs when a caregiver becomes emotionally, socially, mentally and sometimes physically exhausted, resulting in apathy or lack of ability, willingness or energy to provide further attention and care. This is a natural response to the upheaval associated with especially chronic or intense situations and withdrawal is no exception.

It can be difficult for family, friends, doctors and other caregivers to fully understand the effects of withdrawal. No amount of empathy can prepare them for the impact of the physical and psychological symptoms, personality changes and emotional challenges, as well as the practical support which may be required. It is not unusual for them to allude to an overreaction or to the medication causing some form of permanent mental or physical disorder. Because of this, it requires unconditional acceptance to support someone going through withdrawal. This also includes those who are still on the medication and may be experiencing tolerance symptoms, as well as those who may take the drug erratically and are unknowingly experiencing inter-dose withdrawal. It is not only in the acute stages that support is needed.

If you care for someone in withdrawal and are experiencing some or all of the following, you may be at risk of becoming burnt out:

- feeling tired, drained and lethargic
- feeling overwhelmed, constantly worried and helpless
- having frequent headaches and other minor physical complaints
- feeling agitated or easily irritated
- feeling sad and hopeless
- overeating or loss of appetite
- sleep difficulty or oversleeping
- loss of interest in activities previously enjoyed.

TIPS

These tips, if adhered to, will help you to cope better, provide the required support and not become fatigued:

- *Learn more about withdrawal and what it entails.* The more knowledgeable you are about withdrawal, the better prepared you will be to cope with its stages and idiosyncrasies. You will find that you are more understanding and accepting of the person's experience and will be well equipped to give the support needed.

- *Give unconditionally.* You may have your own ideas regarding how withdrawal should be dealt with and what coping strategies and treatment are appropriate. As much as you may be able to empathize, you will not know what the person is going through. Resist suggesting visits to psychiatrists, accelerating or slowing tapers, reinstating the drug, querying other diagnoses such as chronic fatigue syndrome, multiple sclerosis, lupus, depression, fibromyalgia, irritable bowel syndrome or a mental breakdown, and allow the time and space required to heal. Leave it up to him or her to direct you and say what is needed.

- *Withhold judgement.* The true effects of antidepressants, sleeping pills and other benzo tranquillisers are understated and many people find it difficult to accept that taking a legally prescribed drug could result in such adverse reactions. Try to be open and not make judgements based on assumptions or what you perceive to be credible. Even many well-intentioned medics are unaware and uneducated about the full repercussions of this type of dependency and withdrawal.

- *Release expectations.* Appreciate that you have no control over the recovery process so that you don't feel responsible or pressured. The withdrawal experience is unique and unpredictable; you may have to provide support for a much longer period than anticipated.

- *Give practical support.* The person you are caring for may be in severe discomfort and feeling extremely lethargic and depleted of energy. Mowing the lawn, cooking, cleaning, shopping and attending to the children can seem like insurmountable tasks during withdrawal. (Parents with young children can have an exceptionally difficult time coping with demands.) Also, for those with intense symptoms, any form of exertion can cause flare-ups. Offering to help with practical matters will make a remarkable difference.

- *Don't suggest 'snapping out of it' or 'pulling oneself together'.* Don't suggest going back to work or volunteering, especially if symptoms are still severe. Don't tell him or her to stop crying, stop being angry or feeling whatever emotion is present. Don't say other people are worse off. Don't ignore the person's distress or pretend that withdrawal is not happening.

- *Listen actively.* Withdrawal can be overwhelming and the person may be feeling traumatized. Talking is therapeutic and some people feel a need to talk about their experience. Follow his or her cues: if you can, listen actively (without judgement or preconception) as feelings and concerns are shared; at other times space or companionable silence may be all that is needed. Remember, too, that non-verbal communication can be powerful and your warmth, acceptance, expressions and body language are even more important than your words.

- *Don't take things personally.* If the person you are caring for is agitated or becomes angry and overly sensitive, try not to take it personally. The effects of withdrawal can cause mood swings, organic fear, paranoia and a host of other psychological symptoms. Understanding that these reactions are normal will allow you to accept them for what they are while you continue to give your support.

- *Look after yourself well.* Eat healthily, exercise regularly, maintain your hobbies, and get the rest and relaxation you need. Set limits and commit to what is realistic, rather than feel obligated to deliver on promises you are unable to keep, as this will drain you even more. If possible, arrange a respite or back-up person who is reliable and trustworthy so that you can take regular breaks.

- *Get emotional support.* Caring for someone in withdrawal can be mentally draining, so you need to ensure that you take care of your own emotional needs and receive adequate support at this time. It is also important that you have a trusted friend or relative with whom to discuss your fears, needs and feelings. If you become emotionally drained and fatigued, you will have nothing left to give.

- *Reassure, reassure, reassure.* More than anything, someone experiencing withdrawal needs reassurance. Persistent, intense symptoms can cause doubt and increased anxiety. You will need to keep encouraging and reassuring your loved one that recovery is taking place. Hope is one of the most valuable coping tools and your attitude can make a big difference.

- *Keep in touch.* Keep in contact even when it seems the person has recovered. Withdrawal symptoms often come in 'waves' and you may mistake a period during which the symptoms temporarily subside for complete recovery. Many people are devastated when the symptoms resurface and this is when you may be needed the most.

By giving adequate and appropriate support you are making a valuable positive difference to your loved one's withdrawal experience. Your contribution can be one of the most important factors in determining how well she or he copes, and will always be very much appreciated.

ACKNOWLEDGEMENT

If you have the support of family members or friends, please keep in mind how traumatic this experience may indeed be for them too. Withdrawal can make one so self-absorbed that it is easy to overlook the pain, frustration and feelings of helplessness your loved ones have to cope with, along with providing your care. As often as you can, let them know how much you appreciate their assistance and attention.

I often hear from people who are housebound and totally isolated with no one – no family, no friends – to talk to or visit them. You are fortunate. Please don't take the support you receive for granted. Remember to acknowledge the efforts of your loved ones, and when you can, make it your turn to reassure them that the situation is temporary, that you will get better and that life for all of you will eventually return to normal.

11 SUICIDAL IDEATION

Suicide is still a taboo subject with much associated ignorance and stigma. This often results in the reluctance of many who feel suicidal to seek assistance. The fear of being regarded as 'crazy' can make a person in crisis not reach out for help. Even in cases where allusions to having suicidal ideation are made – *I wish I could go to sleep and never wake up* – people may hesitate to ask if suicidal thoughts are present out of concern that they are 'putting ideas' in the person's head. This is not the case. Asking the question is a good way of giving permission to talk and makes it easier for those at risk to share their feelings.

Withdrawal brings with it many physical and emotional challenges which can lead to prolonged low moods. It is understandable that having unrelenting symptom after symptom can be difficult and often makes recovery seem less than a remote possibility. In addition, antidepressant use can have a paradoxical suicidal effect.

It is important to remember that withdrawal is indeed temporary and despite the symptoms, recovery is taking place. However, if a person is already feeling suicidal, hearing this may not help to alleviate the depressive moods and feelings of hopelessness.

In addition, having unwanted repetitive, intrusive thoughts, including those of taking one's life, sometimes accompanied by an obsession with death, can occur during withdrawal. These are either directly or indirectly due to the abnormal reaction caused by the temporary damage to the receptors as a result of long-term use of the drug.

If you are able to identify the thoughts as being due to withdrawal and feel no urge to act on them, they will eventually pass. In the meantime, speaking to someone who is trained to listen actively as often as you need will make coping easier. However, if at all there is an urge to act, you must seek help immediately.

RESOURCES VERSUS ABILITY TO COPE

Regardless of the reasons for having suicidal ideation, the reality is that the emotional and possibly physical pain associated with the experience will have exceeded the resources available. This perceived inability to cope results in a desperate wish to find another way out. Many people give warning signs hoping that someone will care enough to notice and offer help. It does not mean they are mentally ill or weak in any way. They simply feel that they can no longer cope; not even that they want to die, just that they don't believe they have the strength and resources they need to be able to continue. They want to stop their emotional pain.

HELP IS AVAILABLE

If, for whatever reason, you are feeling that you can no longer cope with your situation, there is another way. If you are isolated with no friends or family around, there are people who genuinely care and want to help. Please don't burden yourself by trying to cope with this challenge alone. Help is only a phone call away.

You do not need to act on your impulses right away. A thought is a thought and nothing more; it does not have to lead to action. Talking with someone who will not judge you and is experienced in dealing with crises such as yours will help and you will feel the pressure being relieved. Please consider speaking to a friend or family member or contact an emergency helpline.

WHAT TO DO IF SOMEONE IS SUICIDAL

If you are reading this because a friend or family member has expressed an urge to end his or her life, you could:

- Find out if a plan has been made in terms of what will be used (pills, etc.), at what time and where.

- Make a safety contract with the person: one in which she or he promises to stay safe and not act on any thoughts until a certain time (usually until someone is able to be physically present); that he or she will contact a trained mental health professional, a doctor or hospital if the thoughts and urge persist. Even a promise to phone a designated family member or friend for immediate help is better than having the person on his or her own. Ideally you would stay with the person either on the phone or in person until help arrives.

- Not argue, judge or try to talk the person out of it. She or he is consumed with pain and is feeling emotionally overwhelmed and helpless. This is a time to listen without judgement and to be supportive. Listen for as long as is needed and allow the person to talk, cry, say nothing, vent – whatever it takes. Talking will bring relief from loneliness, release pent up feelings and cause a reduction in agitation.

- Not allow yourself to be sworn to secrecy. There is a reason that mental health professionals exclude 'harm to self or others' from confidentiality clauses. Your friend or family member may be angry with you but at least will be alive.

- Form a 24-hour suicide watch. This can be done discreetly, if necessary, by having family members or friends (who are grounded and capable) take turns to be present throughout the day and night.

- Remove all known means of carrying out the act, including car keys, razor blades, knives, firearms, pills, etc., from easy access.

- Encourage the person to speak to a medical professional or helpline worker.

Examples of distorted thoughts associated with suicidal ideation include:

'I can't see my way out.'

'I can't make the sadness go away.'

'I can't see a future without pain.'

'I can't cope anymore.'

OPEN-ENDED QUESTIONS

If you are concerned about someone who you feel may be having suicidal thoughts, there are ways of conversing that can lead the person to talking through the problem. This is a gentler approach than asking direct questions which may cause the person to become defensive or retreat. Furthermore, not every hunch will be accurate and there are times when a person will be in despair or overwhelmed and not have even the remotest suicidal thought.

An open-ended question (as shown below) rather than a closed-ended, yes/no question such as 'Are you feeling suicidal?' facilitates exploration of feelings. As the person expresses their feelings, there is a reduction in agitation. This allows at least some concerns to be processed, often to a point of emotional safety. A distressed person can sometimes be in conflict or at odds with his or her thoughts and feelings. These types of questions are non-confrontational and give more scope.

Examples of open-ended questions are:

'Can you tell me what you mean by that?'

'How did you feel when that happened?'

'When did you realize it was affecting you so badly?'

'What would be another option for you?'

'What do you think would happen if you did that?'

'ATTENTION-SEEKING' MYTH

If someone hints at wanting to commit suicide, please do not judge or make any assumptions. Discounting the importance of what has been shared with you by thinking the person is being melodramatic is not useful. Even if you conclude that the person is 'attention-seeking', please still go ahead and give the attention needed. It is better to be supportive and not have regrets.

I once pleaded with someone to get help for her teenage son, who I sensed was at high suicide risk; unfortunately, he was instead reprimanded for wanting attention. A few months later he took his life. I feel strongly about this issue. You will never truly know the authentic state of another's emotions. When a person mentions suicide it is usually because urgent attention is needed. It is always wise to take him or her seriously and offer support.

Here are some of the criteria used to identify suicidal risk:

- Recurrent thoughts of or preoccupation with death.

- Recurrent or ongoing suicidal ideation without any plans, or ongoing suicidal ideation with a specific plan.

- Recent suicide attempt, history of depression or history of suicide attempts that required intervention.

- Positive family history of depression and/or a preoccupation with suicidal thoughts.

- Self-destruction or dangerous behaviour (such as reckless driving) which appears to invite death.

- Self-inflicted injuries such as burns and cuts.indirect statements such as 'I can't go on much longer' or 'This voice in my head wants me to do something crazy.'

- Giving away possessions.

DEBRIEFING

Exposure to this kind of situation can be emotionally taxing for the person handling the crisis. It is therefore advisable to have some form of debriefing. This will help to avoid vicarious trauma and other effects such as negatively judging the way the incident was handled. In an informal setting, one way of doing this can be to telephone a crisis helpline and speak to a worker. Without disclosing personal information, you can say what you did, share what you wished you had or had not said, how you felt you did and how you are feeling at the time of the conversation. This is not done for feedback but simply to help you deal with any difficult, residual feelings or uncomfortable emotions that may have arisen.

Finding someone to talk to who, without judgement, can facilitate the honest and frank exploration of difficult feelings will provide immediate relief from distress. If, for whatever reason, you are experiencing suicidal ideation, please seek help. Conversely, if you suspect that someone is having thoughts of taking his or her life, please consider offering help.

12 COUNSELLORS

Counselling during withdrawal can be extremely useful provided the therapist is fully aware of how complex the process is and how it manifests. If not, it will be counterproductive and may even be harmful to the client. Unless the counsellor understands the link between the reversible receptor damage and the client's psychological symptoms, it is likely that any therapeutic approach or treatment plan will be ineffective.

I write from the perspectives of both a service user and provider of services. Attempting to treat a client in withdrawal with only basic knowledge of chemical dependency results in misdiagnoses and causes additional trauma. *Recovery Road* receives calls of this nature regularly from concerned clients who are given inappropriate treatment. Consulting a therapist who is knowledgeable about withdrawal will, on the other hand, empower the client and facilitate a more manageable experience.

COUNSELLING DURING WITHDRAWAL

There were times during withdrawal when I wished I could find a counsellor who understood this type of dependency. I knew from my own training background that there was limited content on antidepressants and benzodiazepines in even the chemical dependency modules of most counselling training programmes. The focus was mainly on alcohol, nicotine and illicit drugs. I was therefore reluctant to consult any professional who was not aware of the full dynamics of withdrawal syndrome.

When my neurologist ruled out withdrawal as the cause of the drug-induced dyskinesia, apart from medication, I was offered CBT. I was first referred to the neuropsychiatry department of the hospital where I underwent a lengthy mental status examination. The neuropsychiatrist concluded that I had handled my withdrawal sensibly and was coping well. She felt that therapy would not help and seemed puzzled that I had been referred to her in the first place.

Despite her observations, a few weeks later I received an information package in preparation for my 'proposed six-week inpatient stay' at the hospital's psychiatric wing. I was deeply perturbed and quickly telephoned an ex-colleague and dear friend who is an experienced and brilliant psychotherapist. I pleaded with her to honestly tell me if she had concerns regarding any aspect of my behaviour. She had been checking on me frequently throughout my post-acute withdrawal period and had witnessed most of the symptoms. Like the neuropsychiatrist, she felt I was very much in awareness of the processes taking place and was coping exceptionally well. We agreed that it would be detrimental to my recovery to be admitted to the hospital. I wrote as gracious a letter as I could muster, thanking them for the care I was given. I then avoided further consultations.

My concern was whether or not the mental health professionals would have acknowledged my symptoms as being due to withdrawal and, consequently, would I be treated with medication that would exacerbate my problems, hinder recovery or create further dependency issues. Having since communicated with thousands of other antidepressant and benzo users, I am tempted to hug myself for my adamancy. When I hear of their experiences with cocktails of medicines many of them were prescribed, I know I made the right decision.

The immediate need for a client in withdrawal is to relate the experience to a non-judgemental listener with the objective of finding ways of coping. A well-meaning counsellor who is not knowledgeable about antidepressants and benzodiazepines will inevitably identify reasons other than withdrawal for the psychological symptoms. This is only due to a lack of awareness and training and is not intentional. Still, it does not help that the client who is struggling to cope with the immediacy of the withdrawal effects may then be asked to explore childhood or relationship issues. This probing therapy can be overwhelming and emotionally damaging to someone who is neurologically over-stimulated, emotionally fragile and vulnerable.

In addition, emotional anaesthesia – the inability to feel pleasure or pain – is a common withdrawal effect. This makes processing and exploration of feelings futile. If a person is unable to access authentic feelings due to the drug's effect, what is there to be processed? It is this point in question that renders counselling during withdrawal (by a therapist who is unaware of antidepressant and benzo-related issues) inappropriate in many cases. Furthermore, with withdrawal-induced brain fog, dysphoria, depersonalization and derealization, being misunderstood and misinterpreted could cause the client to become frustrated and severely depressed.

WHAT EVERY COUNSELLOR SHOULD KNOW

To treat a client in withdrawal without first acquiring in-depth knowledge of the drug and withdrawal syndrome can result in unintentional harm. A good understanding of the withdrawal effects of antidepressants and benzos – not just general drug use – is essential.

The effects of long-term antidepressant or tranquilliser use results in temporary emotional and cognitive disruption, which manifests in the most bizarre ways. Depersonalization, derealization, organic fear, feelings of impending doom, extremely high anxiety, paranoid ideation, repetitive thoughts, weepiness, emotional bluntness, mood swings and brain fog are just some of the common psychological problems which may be experienced during withdrawal. These symptoms do not only surface in clients with pre-existing anxiety or other psychological challenges. Many who were prescribed the medication for medical conditions with no history of anxiety or depression also experience them. They are temporary, however, and usually disappear with recovery.

When assessing a client in the throes of withdrawal, you may note that many of the criteria used to diagnose mental health disorders are fulfilled. A temporarily damaged nervous system can result in the most peculiar and unexpected psychological symptoms. This makes misdiagnosing a high probability and specified knowledge of these drugs a necessity. If the symptoms surfaced during withdrawal, it is best to consider them as physiological – due to receptor damage – and not the result of a mental health issue. After the client has recovered and all the withdrawal-related symptoms have abated, further assessments of any remaining psychological issues may lead to a more accurate diagnosis and appropriate treatment.

In addition, memory impairment, confusion and lack of concentration are common symptoms. Therapeutic treatment which involves maintaining a train of thought is ineffective; it can also be mentally and emotionally draining for these clients. It is only when the nervous system recovers and cognitive faculties improve that exploration and processing will work.

A client may have deep emotional problems which are not related to the drug. They could have been the reason for which the drug was first prescribed. With discontinuance, these issues may resurface. Because of the complexities of long-term use and withdrawal, it will be impossible to determine what is withdrawal-related and what is not, while symptoms are present. Again, it is in the best interest of the client to wait until post-recovery when the accompanying symptoms have subsided to address the pre-existing or underlying issues.

Anyone in withdrawal will benefit most from active listening, constant reassurance and empowerment through the learning of coping skills. Probing and processing of deep emotional problems should be postponed until after the repair of the damage caused by the drug. This will be achieved in due course and normal brain function will return. The client will recover and any psychological symptoms caused by withdrawal will disappear. Should there be any post-traumatic issues or return of an underlying psychological problem post-recovery, then an appropriate counselling or psychotherapeutic approach will certainly be beneficial.

13   DOCTORS

While many doctors and other health care professionals are becoming more knowledgeable about dependency and withdrawal issues related to the long-term use of tranquillisers and antidepressants, others are still quite unaware and may consequently give substandard care, often putting their patients' safety at risk. This information is gleaned mainly from our communication with the thousands of people who have used our services, and so we sincerely hope that it will be considered valid, and that it will help our doctors to better understand the concerns of patients experiencing withdrawal.

WHAT PATIENTS WISH THEIR DOCTORS KNEW

Long-term drug use can result in dependency, with the patient experiencing a myriad of withdrawal symptoms when the drug is discontinued. This withdrawal experience is unique and symptoms vary according to the individual. Common physical symptoms for both antidepressants and benzodiazepines include: zaps, profuse sweating, headaches, nausea, dizziness, gastric disturbances, palpitations, chills, muscle pain and burning, twitches, spasms and tremors. Psychological symptoms, such as feelings of depersonalization, derealization, anxiety, panic attacks, cognitive 'fog' and distorted visual, tactile, auditory and gustatory perception, are also common.

There is nothing more reassuring to a patient than to have his or her doctor confirm that the bizarre symptoms are indeed due to withdrawal, and that they will disappear once withdrawal is over. Sadly, this does not always happen and many patients with no pre-existing psychological problems end up being misdiagnosed and treated for schizophrenia, bipolar and other mental health disorders.

To distinguish between withdrawal and other issues, or return of an underlying condition, the following are good indicators:

- The symptoms will have surfaced during or after tapering or while in tolerance withdrawal.

- Diagnostic tests will be negative.

- Medical symptoms will usually be present as well, and they would have appeared around the same time as the psychological ones.

- The patient will describe a 'chemical feel' to the symptoms which they will say feels nothing like they experienced before.

- Reinstating the drug gets rid of the symptoms.

'COLD TURKEY'

I often hear from individuals who were taken off their medication abruptly and suffer distressing and sometimes dangerous withdrawal reactions. A patient should never be advised to discontinue taking an antidepressant or benzodiazepine abruptly or on a rapid detoxification programme. 'Then stop taking it', was the reply of a well-intentioned doctor when I expressed my concern that the drug had lost its efficacy. Fortunately, I found the *Ashton Manual* and was able to wean off safely and successfully. It is surprising that many doctors still give this advice. Quitting 'cold turkey' is dangerous and can cause serious problems including seizures and psychosis.

TAPERING

The patient must be allowed to taper off the drug at a comfortable pace using the most appropriate weaning process. Short-term-use patients (2–4 weeks) are usually able to taper successfully within 2–4 weeks. For chronic users, smaller reductions in doses may be necessary closer to the end of the taper. The more common methods are: substituting with diazepam, titration by crushing the tablet into a powder and mixing it with water or milk, and the direct method where the dosage is very slowly reduced.

Factors to be considered include personal circumstances, overall general health, the stressors in the patient's life, stamina, support available and previous experience with drugs. It is most important that the patient feel in control of the process. Apart from the usual withdrawal challenges, being pressured into tapering too quickly can cause additional anxiety and hinder recovery. Most patients are able to taper safely and comfortably if the reduction rate is flexible and is based on their withdrawal reactions and intensity of symptoms.

DURATION

The conflicting reports regarding the duration of withdrawal and whether or not protracted withdrawal exists poses one of the biggest problems for patients. Many of our callers are baffled when their doctors explain that since the drug has already left the body, it is impossible for them to still be experiencing withdrawal. This is misleading. When the benzodiazepine subunits have been down-regulated, the process of resynthesizing and re-externalizing onto the receptor assembly can take weeks, months or longer.

Doctors who are unaware of this usually acknowledge the acute and early post-acute stages of withdrawal. However, once symptoms persist longer, these patients are told the withdrawal period has ended and the problems are 'all in the head' or due to some other condition. Furthermore, as alternative diagnoses are queried, additional emotional energy is expended awaiting diagnostic test results which are usually negative. When every test is exhausted, again, the suggestion that the problems are psychological and have nothing to do with withdrawal is inevitably made. This does not augur well for the unfortunate patients who then become concerned about the implied possibility of mental health issues, only to find that the symptoms disappear once the protracted period ends.

Knowledgeable doctors will agree that while many people recover within a 6- to 18-month period, it is not uncommon for a percentage of patients to experience symptoms (often interspersed with windows of normality) for 2–3 years, or longer in rare cases.

'PRE-EXISTING ANXIETY' MYTH

Because many patients are prescribed antidepressants and benzodiazepines for anxiety and mood-related issues, the consensus is usually that any protracted symptoms are in fact due to a resurgence of the pre-existing condition. I was prescribed a benzodiazepine for a neuromuscular condition and had no history of anxiety, depression or any other psychological problem. The anxiety I experienced, especially during acute withdrawal, was inconceivable. *Recovery Road* hears from many people who were also prescribed antidepressants and benzodiazepines for medical problems, yet they experience the most intense organic fear and numerous other psychological symptoms. Pre-existing issues or not, a temporarily compromised nervous system due to withdrawal can reduce the most grounded and stable person to literally a 'quivering wreck'.

It is the responsibility of every doctor who prescribes an antidepressant or benzodiazepine to give the patient information on which the decision to take or not take the drug can be based. When treating patients for anxiety, depression, insomnia or other related conditions, a doctor might understandably be hesitant and conclude that imparting too much information will only make matters worse. However, keeping patients ignorant of the addictive properties of a drug is not in their best interest. It is the reason so many are unpleasantly surprised and left reeling by an unanticipated and devastating withdrawal experience.

14 EMPLOYMENT AND DEBT

EMPLOYMENT

The stress of having to work during withdrawal can worsen symptoms. Some people with mild and tolerable ones are able to continue working. Others are too unwell and end up being temporarily disabled and housebound. An unfortunate percentage who are the sole earners in their families are challenged with the struggle of working throughout the recovery process. These are some of the ways in which withdrawal can affect work:

- increased periods of absenteeism and sick leave

- impaired performance and productivity

- poor timekeeping

- tendency to lose concentration

- tendency to become confused

- memory impairment

- mood swings, irritability or aggression

- low energy or lethargy

- deterioration in relationship with colleagues and clients

- risks of accidents with jobs which involve driving, the use of machinery or dangerous equipment.

Many people in withdrawal are faced with the dilemma of whether or not they should mention the prescribed drug dependency and, if yes, how much they should disclose. Do they risk the possibility of having to deal with the stigmas attached to antidepressant and tranquilliser use and explain about withdrawal? Do they accept other diagnoses such as generalized anxiety disorder or depression in order to obtain approved sick leave? Those with troubling physical symptoms which mimic conditions such as irritable bowel and chronic fatigue syndromes may tend to prefer a medical rather than psychological diagnosis. I am aware of cases where patients accept any misdiagnosis and will not argue with their doctors when told the symptoms can no longer be regarded as withdrawal related, in order to get time off from work.

How a withdrawal-related work issue is managed is often determined by the employer–employee relationship and the organization's health and safety policies. Those who are unable to take time off from work will benefit from having an understanding employer who will allow flexibility in work conditions. Having the minimum number of stressors at this time is the most important factor, and coping with a troubling withdrawal could necessitate extended sick leave, reduction in work hours or a transfer to a less demanding post. Bearing in mind that withdrawal does not normally last indefinitely, any action taken will be temporary. Once you are recovered, you will be able to resume work. Having overcome this challenge, you may even end up feeling confident and inspired enough to embark upon a new career.

Ultimately, successfully coping with withdrawal and achieving recovery should be the priority. Having an income is important, but if working interferes with your recovery process, you will need to assess the advantages to determine whether or not they are worth the resultant hindrances.

DEBT

One of the often overlooked repercussions of having a long, protracted withdrawal is financial difficulty. Apart from being disabling, a troubling withdrawal can cause vulnerability to debt problems. As we are already aware, a combination of physically and psychologically impairing symptoms can cause an inability to work or a reduction in work hours for some.

There are many cases of people who, at the unexpected onset of acute withdrawal, are thrown into a period of personal crisis without the capacity to attend to their financial concerns. This causes a rapid accumulation of debt problems and the person can be so unwell and cognitively impaired that she or he is unaware or unable to seek advice or claim state benefits. Demands from unsympathetic creditors, job loss, inability to pay the mortgage and fear of losing one's home are just a few of the additional financial issues that can present with withdrawal and contribute to higher levels of anxiety.

As we know, although temporary, withdrawal can persist for much longer than anticipated. In many cases, being granted state benefits specifically for withdrawal can be difficult and, in this situation, settling for depression or an anxiety-related diagnosis may be regarded as an acceptable alternative.

If you are experiencing financial difficulties as a result of withdrawal, you are entitled to assistance in the form of advice and benefits. Your claim is legitimate and should be regarded as no different to those of patients with other disabilities.

Should you be concerned about stigmatization or prejudicial judgements in the case of advice regarding your debt problems, you will need to weigh this against the toll that the stress of being in debt will take on your health. Your recovery should take precedence over every other issue.

With regard to state benefits, your first claim may be declined and you may have to reapply or appeal. Please do not let this deter you. Keep persisting and you will succeed. If you are incapable of completing the arduous process, there are voluntary organizations and agencies, such as the Citizens Advice Bureau (UK) as well as withdrawal-support charities, that will provide the necessary information, advice and assistance with applications.

Try not to allow financial difficulties to overwhelm you. Do what you can to get the assistance you need. If your symptoms are problematic and your cognition is impaired, get a trusted family member, friend or a support agency to help you to assess your circumstances and to contact your debtors. It is important to do this as soon as you realize there is a problem, as ignoring the issue will only worsen the situation and increase your anxiety. More than anything, keep in mind that withdrawal is temporary. If you have had to give up work completely or reduce your hours, take comfort in knowing that with recovery you will regain your health, your capacity for earning, and the ability to improve your financial situation.

15   RECOVERY

Recovery has a different meaning to each of us. Some people wait for every symptom to go, others begin to celebrate when the most troubling symptoms disappear and the remaining ones are bearable, and some consider themselves mostly recovered when they are able to resume normal activities – even with residual symptoms. The moment I noticed I stopped having brain fog, other cognitive issues and just a few physical symptoms remained, I told myself my recovery had at last arrived. I continued to improve for a long time after and am now fully recovered as I write, but this was the beginning of a celebration that continues even today.

No matter what stage of withdrawal you may be at while reading this, always keep trusting that recovery is the natural outcome of the process. It is inevitable that your receptors will one day be up-regulated and will begin to work efficiently again at keeping your nervous system calm and moods balanced. This is the time when all your symptoms will disappear for good and you will prepare for your new beginning. Even if the process is taking longer than you anticipated, always remind yourself that one day you, too, can be expected to be celebrating the end of this journey.

The following logs were written after I had my final wave of symptoms. I hope the insights will spur you on and encourage you while you wait for your own recovery journey to be completed.

JOURNAL LOGS

December 17, 2007

TWO-YEAR BENZO-FREE ANNIVERSARY

Today is a significant day for me. In late 2003 I found the *Ashton Manual* online. That marked the beginning of my healing. I then survived a chaotic series of bizarre events spanning a four-year period. They all turned out to be miraculously synchronized and unfolded in perfect order. I am pleased to acknowledge today as being exactly two years since I have been benzo-free.

Yes, two years ago today, I took my last tiny piece of diazepam. Five months earlier, on July 17, 2005, I took my last clonazepam. I have no hesitation in saying that coming off the medication is one of the best decisions I have ever made.

Withdrawal, however challenging it may be, is worth enduring when it results in the clarity, coherence and general wellness that I am currently experiencing.

Even with the residual protracted symptoms, I feel 100 per cent better than I did two years ago. And, compared to when I was still on the medication and in tolerance withdrawal, I feel 200 per cent better.

I admit that there are times when I have felt a bit impatient because I want all the symptoms to go so I can pronounce myself 'fully recovered'. All I do then is think of how much improved I am. In reality, I am more than fully recovered because I've got the old 'me' back, the person I almost completely lost during the tolerance years, long before tapering. *Every day in every way I am getting better and better. I am grateful for my healing.*

January 1, 2008

CLARITY

Today I looked at a photo taken outside my front gate. Although I had always savoured the river's serenity, until recently I had not noticed the ripples in the water. During the bad withdrawal days I would sit outside my door and look at the swans, ducks, birds and weeping willows. It was therapeutic. Now that the depersonalization, derealization, brain fog and spaciness have gone, I know that I wasn't able to fully interact or appreciate the beauty through my then blurred eyes and blunt emotions. What I am seeing now is breathtaking; what I am feeling is profound and authentic.

Today, for the first time since tolerance withdrawal, long before I tapered off the clonazepam, I am aware of how much more I am able to truly connect with my surroundings. It feels almost overwhelming to see vivid colours and notice details that were always present but my veiled eyes could not see, at least not through the fog.

I know some of you are still having a difficult time with no windows yet. Sometimes I am hesitant about being too jubilant about my recovery because I do not want to appear insensitive. I do not want you to think I am discounting the fact that it is challenging for you at this time. But I also know that there were times when anyone who was benzo-free and had good news to share would give me more hope in terms of my own healing. This is what I want to achieve by sharing my positive observations. This clarity is worth looking forward to.

In November, when I was dizzy all the time and having an intense setback, I goaded myself into being patient with no timeline for my recovery. A few months later, I am enjoying this feeling of having 'restored' vision. It is like seeing the world through new eyes.

January 11, 2008

PROSPERITY

Often when we read of people's withdrawal experiences they mention losing everything; I can relate to that. I made a lot of unsound decisions that had devastating repercussions financially but to be benzo-free and resuming a normal life makes it more than worth it.

As withdrawal began to affect me during my second attempt at tapering, I decided to leave the UK and sold both my home and car at a loss. For a long time I couldn't remember what had happened to my hundreds of CDs, DVDs, books and electronic items. Then recently my friends reminded me that I had asked them to take large boxes filled with thousands of pounds worth of items to charity shops or to give them away to anyone who wanted them. They had wondered what was wrong with me at the time. An ex-neighbour told me I had left my front door open and invited them to take all my brand new furniture, appliances and anything else they wanted. I don't remember.

During withdrawal I lived off my savings until my accounts were depleted, then family and friends helped to support me. When I returned close to the end of acute withdrawal, my first few months were spent in bed. I was deep in the throes of withdrawal and felt ill all the time. I could not sit up for more than ten or 15 minutes at a time. I was staying with a friend, had two bags with a few clothes, three little teddy bears, and my laptop. I had lost everything. I remember thinking, *How did this happen? Where's my stuff? What do I do now? How do I start over?* The withdrawal symptoms were so severe, I knew there was no way I could go out to work. I had to find a way of coping and continued to use positive self-talk, visualization, affirmations and other techniques to remain optimistic.

Then there was a shift. Something changed and it was liberating. I had nothing external to identify with – no job, no home, no spouse, nothing. I had nowhere to go. I couldn't hop on a plane, I couldn't even go for a walk. But I had 'me' and I was alive. I found a lot of other things to be grateful for. It was empowering, like an awakening, and I began to see my experience as a specially wrapped gift that was priceless. I knew that I would emerge better off physically, mentally, spiritually, emotionally and financially. I didn't need to know how, I just knew.

Today, I am re-acquiring necessities. I seem to need a lot less than I used to, and life is simpler but richer. What matters most is that I have clarity of mind and a nervous system that is beginning to function normally – something no amount of money can buy. Prosperity is about abundance in every area of our lives and I am grateful that I have more than enough of everything I need.

January 16, 2008

POSITIVES ABOUT WITHDRAWAL

It is good to keep remembering that every symptom is evidence that your nervous system is healing. It is readjusting to being fully functional without the drug. You are going through this to get to that place of recovery. Symptoms are symbolic of the recovery process.

If you have not been able to work, it allows you to get a well-deserved break from the rat-race. You get an opportunity to re-evaluate your work aspirations and even make plans for a career change post-recovery, if that is what you have decided you want.

You may have found that at least one person has turned out to be the most supportive, loyal and non-judgemental friend or family member that anyone could ever ask for. If you have lost connections with others who were unable to support you for whatever reasons, you now have more space in your life to welcome new, meaningful relationships – which you will.

You may have gained confidence as well as renewed respect for your body for having endured withdrawal. You may find that once you are over the shock of the experience, you will have a sense of invincibility and no challenge will ever again faze you.

You may find that the withdrawal experience has made you tap into your spirituality and has re-ignited your relationship with and belief in a God, Higher Power, Source, Spirit – whatever name you use or concept you have. You now have an unshakable faith and will approach any future obstacles with confidence.

It is possible that you are now *au fait* with coping strategies, techniques, alternative therapies, healthy eating, exercise, and are on your way to being fitter and more balanced in mind, body and spirit than you were before. You have become a 'Walking Wikipedia' or reference library, well-equipped to help yourself and others.

Things are no longer taken for granted. You may notice feeling pleased and grateful for being able to accomplish a simple task or hobby that at one point, during the worst of withdrawal, you doubted you would ever be able to do again.

If you are experiencing withdrawal, it means you are on your way to creating a new beginning. You can look forward to being benzo-free, to having a clear, lucid mind, a strong, retentive memory, being focused and able to concentrate. Your cognition will no longer be impaired and you will feel like a new person. Being in withdrawal means you are preparing for a new healthy reality that will give stability, clarity and purpose, and make you open to receiving your good.

THE AFTERMATH

February 10, 2008

FROM WINDOWS TO OPEN DOOR

I am writing this for anyone who is still trying to cope with the brain fog, depersonalization, derealization and other psychological and physical symptoms. I am thankful for my current window of clarity which I think has become my open door to recovery. It has now been ten weeks. The continuous lucidity and clarity of thought are still slightly unfamiliar. It feels pleasantly strange after having spent the last ten years in a blurred reality. My recovery still makes me feel emotional and extremely pleased. I feel as if I have been given a second chance at life.

Not very long ago, I was having one of my worst withdrawal waves. Despite affirming and remaining positive, there was a tiny part of me that wondered whether I should just accept that I may just be the most unfortunate person in the world – that I may have a few more years to wait for my recovery. A little voice tried to reason that maybe it was part of my reality, a path I needed to take, and if I affirmed otherwise, it was my ego getting in the way. I resisted those fears and continued affirming my healing and speaking positively to myself. A bigger voice inside responded saying, 'Be patient; you will make your own happy ending.'

I started challenging myself to do a lot of the activities I had postponed for when I got better – anything that I was capable of doing. I stopped giving attention to the symptoms, acting, even if in mind only, as if I had no symptoms. This was difficult with the dizziness and hearing problems but there was a part of me that just would not give in to that other voice telling me withdrawal has gone on for much too long and it must be something more.

If any of this resonates with you, I cannot tell you with any more conviction that your healing is taking place, now, as you read this. When a symptom seems unrelenting and you have done everything possible and nothing seems to be working, trust that your brain is in the process of readjusting to being functional without the drug. Then imagine what you will be like (go into as much detail as possible and feel it as well) without the foggy brain or whatever your symptoms are. See yourself doing all the things you cannot yet do but will be able to when the symptoms go.

When I read what I had written in November and think of how I feel now, I cannot help but write to remind you that every day in every way your body is recovering. Your healing has already taken place.

April 19, 2008

RELATIONSHIPS

When I think of my relationships – those that survived, those I have lost and new ones I have made, I have no regrets. I think about my caring, loyal family members and friends who supported me throughout the tolerance and withdrawal years, and am overcome with deep gratitude. I feel so honored to have had their attention and care. I do not know how I would have coped otherwise.

I also think about others who found my experience too much to cope with and avoided contact. In some cases I did too, as I did not have the emotional energy to expend at the time. Coping simultaneously with withdrawal and the more demanding relationships can be emotionally draining. It was necessary for me to let them go. Stress reduction was my objective and it worked. I have released these relationships with love.

If some friends or family members become unavailable and inaccessible during your withdrawal, it could be because they are unable to relate to your experience or they simply cannot cope. You may be able to reconcile some of these relationships after you recover or you may have to lovingly release them from your life. What you will find is a special gift – that of being surrounded by people who genuinely and unconditionally care. You will also find that you are now left with ample space in your life to accommodate new, loving relationships.

I am grateful for the relationships that have been strengthened as a result of my experience, for the new friendships I have made, and for being unconditionally loved and supported. I am grateful too, for my recovery and being able to reciprocate.

May 8, 2008

RACKING MY BRAIN

I keep saying that one day withdrawal will be a distant memory but how do I know this to be true? It is because my lucidity, coherence, cognitive faculties and physical stamina have been so fully restored that hard as I try, I can barely recall what having brain fog and all the other symptoms was like.

Today I will reiterate the fact that no matter where you are in your recovery process, the day will come when you will once again feel well. You will be so busy resuming your normal activities, you won't give withdrawal a thought, or you will have to struggle to remember what it was like.

I vaguely remember what my days of tolerance, acute and protracted withdrawal were like. I read through my journals and old logs and have very little recollection with no negative emotions. I know that for a brief period late in my recovery stage I recognized some strong post-traumatic type emotions. I felt shell-shocked and kept thinking, *How on earth did this happen to me?* But along with my physical healing my spirit has healed and is lighter than before, and now I celebrate the content, grounded, post-withdrawal me. You will too.

You may be experiencing brain fog, adrenaline surges, feelings of depersonalization and derealization, distorted visual or tactile perception and other psychological and physical withdrawal symptoms. In a few months or possibly (but hopefully not) years, you will look back at this time and think, *I can't remember what withdrawal was like.*

I have been writing online for more than a year. I smile when I think that some of my withdrawal friends who were distraught about their unrelenting symptoms and emailed me for many months are fully recovered. They are preoccupied with their families, back at work, or so busy in general that I either don't hear from them or I get a keep-in-touch email once in a while.

I am always pleased when a regular visitor stops logging on to this site because it is no longer necessary. Quite a few of our benzo friends whose relationships ended because of the benzo issue have met new people. One gentleman emailed me today to say he has met someone new and is engaged to be married.

I know it can be challenging at times to see past your withdrawal experience. Please remember that benzo withdrawal is a syndrome and not a medical condition for which you will need continuous treatment. It is temporary, with a positive outcome. It will strengthen your character and resolve, your nervous system will recover and be restored to full functionality. You will, one day, have to rack your brains to remember what your experience was like. If you are feeling discouraged, please keep these thoughts in mind.

May 19, 2008

ALL IS WELL

I am pleased to share that I am still enjoying my recovery with no recurrence of withdrawal symptoms. I keep improving daily and feel better than I have in many years. Withdrawal waves and windows are no more. It has been an open door into the world of coherence and lucidity for which I am grateful. I know that when the timing is right, you too, will be celebrating your recovery.

I still have the intermittent drug-induced dyskinesia and my hearing remains distorted but I have no complaints. It is pure bliss to have my cognitive faculties back, to be able to complete a sentence, to think clearly and to remember what I am looking for or where I put it.

So, here I am again, the broken record, reminding you that if you are still experiencing withdrawal symptoms, they will go as soon as your receptors are up-regulated and your nervous system has recovered. Like me, you will keep improving until you are fully healed.

June 15, 2008

HOW I KNEW IT WAS OVER

While I can't recall an exact date, here is the sequence of events that led me to the realization that withdrawal was finally over. I had my first, very brief window of clarity early on in withdrawal – approximately two months after the end of my complete taper. It lasted a short time and throughout the next two years a pattern of windows and waves developed.

Close to the end of the second year, along with the spasms and hearing problems, I started having some surprisingly severe waves with extreme dizziness and other symptoms. I knew though, that withdrawal was coming to an end especially because my clarity, coherence and cognitive faculties were significantly improving.

I had to learn to not anticipate a window or wave. I relinquished control and just observed the process, trusting that the outcome would be good. I did not resist and kept reminding myself that in spite of all the madness, all the inconsistencies and surprises, I was recovering. I regarded the disturbances as evidence that my nervous system's fine-tuning was taking place.

Then, around the two-year mark I had influenza and it did not trigger a withdrawal wave as would have been the case during the first 18 months of withdrawal. For the next few months the window continued and I was more lucid and coherent than I had been throughout the tolerance and withdrawal years. It was a gradual observation. I felt that if more than three months passed without a wave of symptoms, then surely it must mean recovery. That was indeed the case.

I hope that this will happen for you too. Even if it seems to be taking forever, the brain fog and other symptoms do not usually last indefinitely. The thing about withdrawal is that there is no logic, set pattern, reason or rhyme to it. This is why patience, non-anticipation, non-resistance and hope are our best companions throughout this journey. The only thing we know for certain is that withdrawal is temporary and in time, we recover.

June 17, 2008

THE CALM AFTER THE STORM

There is another dimension to the aftermath of withdrawal. Earlier this year during the first few months of no waves, apart from being elated and relieved, I felt slightly shell-shocked and shaken. Withdrawal for me was like having a category five hurricane arrive without warning and having to run inside for shelter, but instead of it lasting hours it lasted two and a half years.

The windows of clarity were akin to the calm that one experiences when the eye of the storm is passing. The waves of symptoms were the high, destructive winds. All I could do was accept my fate, curl up on the sofa and wait for the fury to subside.

At last the storm passed, and I emerged from the rubble feeling grateful for having survived. I looked at the debris and the material damage but felt no sense of loss because I was alive and well. I was feeling better than I had during the tolerance years when the storm was brewing. I consider that period just after the last wave to be my post-trauma period.

Now, almost six months later, I am still in awe of the clarity, lucidity and physical wellness that I am experiencing. I cannot articulate the sense of peace that my experience has brought me. The many days of not being able to go out or even to read left me with no option but to breathe and be still.

I know that coping with withdrawal is a big challenge. Yet, so far, many of us who have now moved on confirm that withdrawal has set us up for life in terms of the lessons and revelations. Learning patience, compassion and appreciation for the simplest things in life are invaluable gifts.

Most of us do not regret having had this experience because once you have recovered you are inclined to think: *Wow, I survived. I made it. I am amazing. I can handle anything now.* It makes the everyday challenges of life seem insignificant. As one friend who is now recovered said, 'Life after withdrawal is a piece of cake'.

You may be feeling shell-shocked because this experience is so surreal, was not anticipated, and literally threw your equilibrium off. It will help if you are able to relax into the present moment, symptoms and all, and remember that you are being set up for life. When this is over, nothing will faze you.

June 22, 2008

WINDS OF CHANGE

Today is an unusually windy day in South Wales with extremely high gusts. Outside my home are two big weeping willow trees which line the water's edge. I've grown quite attached to them especially to the larger of the two, the branches of which hang near my windows.

I gaze outside and I can see the less flexible trees and other plants losing leaves and branches as they resist the wind, but my dear weeping willows are simply swaying, dancing, moving to and fro, making beautiful music in the process.

As I enjoy the windsong, my mind wanders to the withdrawal experience and I feel moved to write about it. When we go against the wind, we become tense, rigid and more susceptible to the pressure. When we gently ease into the flow and not resist, we are less likely to 'break' and tend to have a smoother emotional path to recovery.

May the winds of your challenge soon take you back to that place of wellness. As your journey progresses, may you be filled with acceptance and courage. May you also have hope, peace and even find opportunities to make good music and dance along the way.

July 3, 2008

WELLNESS IS OUR NATURAL STATE OF BEING

It is now the seventh month of my recovery from benzodiazepine withdrawal. I had no inkling that this adventure of a lifetime would have resulted from my flippantly waltzing into my doctor's office, that morning in 1998, concerned that my dystonic tics would ruin my wedding.

I am still amazed at my body's resilience and its natural ability to heal. Yes, I am still having the involuntary spasms and hearing issues but oh how well I feel, and how much more content I am. Had I not been logging my experience, I would not have remembered much. If you are finding coping with your symptoms challenging, please take heart in what I am writing today.

After having had the brain fog and other cognitive issues during the tolerance years and then the intensification during acute and post-withdrawal, I seriously experienced moments of underlying doubt, and sometimes wondered whether I was in denial and should I not accept that this is how I will be permanently experiencing my new world. (This tends to happen to those whose symptoms persist longer than expected.)

Having worked in the mental health field, I knew that the brain fog and some of the other psychological symptoms form the blurred reality through which many people navigate their daily lives. I thought maybe it was my fate too. I was not depressed or even upset when I had these thoughts, I just wanted to be 'realistic' and non-resistant. I felt inclined to plan how I was going to make the best of a life observed through what seemed like a veil or smoke screen.

Then, January came and the clarity kept improving daily. As the months went by I began to experience my pre-benzo coherence and lucidity. I still find it fascinating that one little pill could make such an impact on every aspect of a person's life. I can never run out of things to be grateful for because every day I have constant reminders of how well-recovered I am.

Yesterday, for the first time since withdrawal, I noticed the ringing in my ears (tinnitus) had stopped. I was agog and at a loss for words. It didn't last long, only about ten minutes, but I was thrilled. Experiencing that intense silence was remarkable. I know that there is a bit more 'repair work' to be done and so I trust that this will be resolved in time.

If you have been waiting for months or even years for the fog to lift and for your psychological and physical symptoms to go, please trust that your recovery is on schedule. Try to be patient and not resist the changes that are taking place. Practise positive self-talk and other coping tools, nurture yourself well, and then sit back and allow the major overhaul (receptor issue) and then fine-tuning to take place. Know that one day, like me, you will be reflecting on the times when you thought you would not have survived, and you will smile and shake your head and think, *Yes, I did it!*

16 CLOSURE

The nightmare has ended. The waves of symptoms gradually became shorter and the windows of clarity longer; or maybe you had very few or no windows and woke up one morning to find all the symptoms gone. Still, you are hesitant to claim your recovery. What if, as in the past, you declare full recovery only to be swept away by another wave? Then you think, 'No, it has been months since I've had a flare-up; this must be it.' Yes, this is it! The moment you have dreamt of for what seemed like forever has finally arrived.

Your precious receptors have been repaired and your nervous system is no longer compromised and struggling to function. Even if one or two symptoms are still persisting, once the waves of intense symptoms have gone and you are feeling well for a prolonged period, there is no harm in claiming your recovery. You can now pronounce yourself recovered. Whether full or incomplete, you can exhale. You are now, once again, in control of your life.

You coped successfully through withdrawal and that means not only are you a survivor, you have proven how strong, courageous and amazing a person you are. This is no time for modesty; withdrawal was a monumental challenge and you've made it through to the very end. Congratulations!

The absence of symptoms, however, is only one aspect of recovery. There may be a few more hurdles to overcome on the way to achieving a genuine state of complete healing. A problematic withdrawal can be so devastating that it is no surprise that letting go of the experience can sometimes be difficult for some.

People react differently to the realization of recovery. After receiving confirmation that withdrawal is over, some are left feeling shell-shocked and traumatized for a while. In an effort to forget the experience others refuse to talk about it or relive it in any way. For them, this is closure. Others spend a long time after recovery trying to come to terms with their losses. They may have lost prime years of their lives, relationships and property; this makes starting over challenging.

Recognizing and processing these losses may be a necessary path to healing. Problems arise when one over-identifies and remains attached to the experience and the associated negative emotions become ingrained in the psyche. This results in an inability to move on. The preoccupation with the withdrawal experience ends up lasting indefinitely, and although the symptoms have permanently subsided, the person continues to feel generally unwell. The ideas shared in the next chapter as well as having counselling can be beneficial for anyone faced with this obstacle.

If you were on both an antidepressant and a tranquilliser, you may be concerned about having to do another taper. Don't worry; you've made it through withdrawal once – you'll definitely survive it the next time around. You are now well prepared for dealing with these issues.

If you plan on promoting awareness about antidepressants and benzodiazepines, it is best to consider doing this after your emotional healing has taken place. The negatives associated with the experience should be released in order for physical and emotional wellness to be maintained. Although withdrawal may have already stolen a few or many years of your life, it is now time to let it go in order to create room for the good that awaits you.

STIGMATIZATION

One aspect of the aftermath of withdrawal which may be surprising is how quickly one can be judged and stigmatized. I remember feeling misunderstood when an old friend immediately recoiled once I shared my experience. She lectured me about being 'on guard' and not 'giving in' to my cravings, then avoided me. This is a typical reaction.

Stigmatization involves labelling someone because of a condition or an experience, stereotyping and devaluing the person. Some people find that despite having been prescribed the drug, acquiring it legally and not having had cravings, they are still subject to the judgement and unfortunate stigma that goes with being considered an addict. This stigmatization (which should not exist in any case) is based on ignorance and lack of awareness and will be perpetuated until antidepressant and tranquilliser issues are acknowledged and addressed.

Although the symptoms that you have experienced were due to withdrawal, many may not regard this as a legitimate medical conclusion. You may, therefore, be judged as creating your withdrawal problems through your own choices and actions. There is nothing to be ashamed of. You were prescribed a drug and were unaware of its effects. Prescribed drug dependency and iatrogenic addiction can affect anyone and any family; no one is exempt.

Again, due to lack of awareness, the magnitude of the issues you have overcome may go unacknowledged and you may not receive the deserved recognition. Don't be perturbed; those of us who have survived withdrawal know that we are remarkably resilient, strong and courageous. We also know stigmatization exists. So, then, how do we cope? First, you are not obligated to share your experience. You can decide how much to disclose and to whom. You may be comfortable speaking to certain family members and friends, or you may decide to talk about it only if absolutely necessary. The most important thing is to not let fear or anticipation of being stigmatized lead to social isolation. Even if you choose not to discuss your experience, it is important to stay in touch with those who care about you. You do not want to end up losing much-needed social interaction and support.

You may, like me, feel extremely proud of overcoming your dependency and surviving withdrawal. This could lead to your decision to actively challenge stigma and to promote awareness within your wider circle of family and friends; or you may opt for tackling the bigger issues by joining the existing 'army' of awareness lobbyists, setting up a website or giving support within the withdrawal community. Energy channelled into promoting awareness, lobbying and supporting others can be beneficial, is badly needed and is always welcome.

RETURN OF UNDERLYING CONDITION

A question which is very frequently asked during withdrawal and after recovery is whether or not the underlying condition for which the drug was prescribed will return. It may have been prescribed for depression or an anxiety-related condition because of a transitory response to a traumatic life event such as a bereavement, and the person ended up taking it for a much longer period than intended. The best scenario is that she or he is pleasantly surprised to find that the underlying condition is gone; this happens quite often. If this is not the case and the underlying condition returns, depending on what it is, there are other options.

Those who were prescribed the drug for chronic anxiety or other psychological issues may now resolve that no matter what lies ahead, they will be able to follow a non-pharmacological route leading to other ways of coping. They may not have been aware of many of these methods prior to taking the drug. What could have once been regarded as too simple solutions – breathing practices, mindfulness, guided imagery, emotional freedom techniques, meditation, progressive relaxation and other self-management tools learned during withdrawal – have become invaluable alternatives. Some become experts at grounding themselves and using positive self-talk to remain calm. Others who are unable to successfully apply these types of self-help techniques find CBT and other forms of counselling to be useful.

Many feel a strong sense of accomplishment after having survived withdrawal. The issue for which the drug was prescribed now seems insignificant in comparison with the multitude of problems faced and conquered during withdrawal. Being able to have successfully dealt with the bizarre physical and psychological symptoms gives them new confidence. If this is not the case for you and you are finding it difficult to cope with a pre-existing condition, please seek help.

LETTING GO

Depending on the duration of your medication use and recovery period, you may be starting over after a very long break from 'normal' life. My withdrawal adventure began in 1998 and I confirmed my recovery in early 2008. When I was first prescribed the drug my waist measured 25 inches, I had fewer wrinkles and I had higher energy levels. Because I was in a fog for most of the 10 years of my experience, I went through a phase post-recovery where I wanted to backtrack and pick up from the spring of 1998. It was not possible and I quickly had to accept that withdrawal or not, I would have had other challenges and I also would have aged! Being realistic is liberating.

If you are a few pounds heavier with little aches and pains, please don't let this prevent you from enjoying your recovery. You may have 'two pack' abdominals instead of a 'six pack', your skin and hair may be different and there may also be a few other unwelcome changes. Despite all of this, you are alive and well and most of all, drug-free. Even if one or two minor symptoms are persisting, you can make the most of the good health that you now enjoy and continue to effect new changes.

REGAINING CONFIDENCE

Not everyone emerges from the withdrawal experience unscathed, and with elevated self-worth. Some feel remorseful and blame themselves for not having been more vigilant. They regret not having researched the drug or asking the initial prescribing doctor more questions. Others think, 'How could I have let this happen?' Please do not let guilt affect your emotional healing.

Still, if there is a need to rationalize, you can consider this: Now that you have been through withdrawal you, more than anyone, are aware of the general lack of awareness regarding antidepressants and benzodiazepines. How then could you, an average layperson, have known about the dependency properties of the drug? It is most likely that you were experiencing a traumatic event or some other serious life situation and needed help. Your intention was not to take a drug that would so negatively affect you and impact your life. You made what seemed to have been the best decision based on the choices and information you were given at the time. You did not 'let it happen'. Please let go of any self-blame you may be feeling. 'It' happened and you beat it. That is all that matters now. This experience is now a proud part of your past.

Now is the time to acknowledge your exceptional accomplishment. What you have just experienced, if seen from a positive perspective, can turn out to be your biggest confidence booster. You made the decision to quit a highly addictive substance. You found the courage and determination to taper. If you cold turkeyed, not only were you brave, you had 'someone' watching over you. You then coped with acute and post-acute withdrawal.

Try not to look outside of yourself for commendation. It is difficult for anyone who has not been through withdrawal to appreciate the magnitude of the challenge and the complex dynamics involved. Whether you have fully or partially recovered from withdrawal, you deserve to have the highest self-esteem possible. If this does not resonate with you, the guidance offered in the next chapter will help.

Wherever your experience takes you, always remember that you have overcome an immense challenge. You have successfully coped with withdrawal and are now once again in control of your life. You do not need to justify what transpired, convince anyone that withdrawal was not 'all in your head', or feel embarrassed or humiliated. You can release any negative aspects of this experience knowing that you are a survivor and an extremely resilient person.

17 YOUR NEW CHAPTER

Your withdrawal chapter is now closed. Although you may have preferred being given the option to press a 'delete' button before it even began, remind yourself that this is not the end of the book. Life continues. Now that the chapter which had the biggest lessons in patience and non-resistance is at last over, it is time to turn the page and begin your new one – a fulfilling chapter, now on your terms.

For those who find it difficult to move on, lack of confidence could be an issue that needs to be addressed. Dealing with month after month of cognitive problems and other psychological withdrawal symptoms may have strongly impacted your self-belief and affected your ability to make self-assured life decisions. The goal here is to help you to identify ways to regain your confidence should this be the case, and for those who already feel dauntless to be further empowered, so that you can create balance and stability to help you move on. Not everything mentioned here will be relevant and some recommendations will appeal more than others, so see which are important to you. If you are still in withdrawal, as soon as you are able, try to incorporate the suggestions that resonate. They will help you to stay as motivated as possible until you are well enough to resume normal life.

HELPFUL SUGGESTIONS
IDENTIFY AND CHALLENGE LIMITING BELIEFS

The first thing you will need to do is identify and understand any limiting beliefs you hold of yourself – possibly as a result of withdrawal or from previous issues – and then examine the evidence and challenge them. For example, you may tell yourself:

> 'Since my withdrawal, I have no friends. No one cares and no one likes me.'

You then challenge this with what you know to be true:

> 'Tommy still cares about my well-being and visits me once a week.'

> 'Dad phoned me yesterday.'

> 'Sue, my new friend from the online support group, likes me very much and we write to each other every day.'

You may end up with a long list and will be surprised to find that most of the beliefs you hold can be quickly disproved. So many of our negative thoughts which we have repeated to ourselves over time eventually become instilled. But they are not factual. Writing these exercises and journaling are always useful because during the times when you may be feeling dejected and lacking in motivation, you can easily and quickly reread your insights and this will give you a confidence boost and energy lift.

FIND THINGS ABOUT YOURSELF THAT YOU LIKE

People sometimes feel resistance when doing this. We have been conditioned by society to be 'humble' and are even encouraged to be self-deprecating. But it is very healthy to acknowledge your positive attributes. You can write about character traits, skills you possess, kind things you do, your good habits, how you look – anything you can think of that is pleasing. For example:

'I genuinely care about others.'

'I am a good singer.'

'I recycle and do my best to reduce my carbon footprint.'

Do this often and, again, keep the list handy so you can read and reread it. You will find that there is much to like and your list will get longer and longer. Get into the habit of speaking to yourself positively, about yourself. This one simple exercise could boost your confidence and bring you closer to feeling you are deserving of good opportunities and contentment.

SET BOUNDARIES

Setting boundaries is one way of valuing yourself and taking personal responsibility. It is not unusual to feel guilty and uncomfortable when saying 'no' to requests from family, friends and colleagues. If you are asked to commit to doing something you are not comfortable with, it is okay to say a firm but gentle 'no'. If you are hesitant or feel you need more information, say, 'I need time to think about this. I will get back to you.' Then ask yourself if you have all the facts needed to make your decision. If not, ask as many questions as necessary.

When you say 'no' make eye contact, be assertive and do not make excuses. If you do not want to do something, don't do it. The exception will be if it involves saving someone's life, in which case you will want to do whatever is necessary. When you are able to say 'no' comfortably, without being aggressive or difficult, you will be confident and pleased with yourself that you are able to set clear boundaries.

SET REALISTIC GOALS

Give yourself challenges that are achievable, starting with the smallest first. Let them be things that are meaningful. For example, you could clear the clutter from your closets and pack a few charity bags. Then you could move on to doing something more challenging. Sharing your intention with someone you trust will make you accountable and you can both acknowledge and celebrate as each goal is accomplished. The more you achieve, the stronger your feelings of self-worth will become and the more you will be motivated to do.

SPEND TIME WITH POSITIVE, SUPPORTIVE PEOPLE

Avoid the people who encourage you to be negative – who complain, criticize, and treat you in ways that could reinforce your misperception of not being worthy. Let go of the relationships that are filled with drama and leave you feeling drained and depressed. Instead, associate with people who are respectful, whose company you find uplifting, who listen to you and validate your feelings.

BE KIND TO YOURSELF

Don't wait for your confidence to increase before you practise being kind to yourself. It can work the other way around too, if you act 'as if'. So the kinder and gentler you are with yourself now, the more deserving you will increasingly feel. Don't put yourself down or compare yourself with others. Accept compliments. Be assertive and don't allow people to treat you with a lack of respect. Nurture yourself and give yourself treats more than occasionally. Be open to receiving and accept opportunities that could lead to positive life experiences.

BE KIND TO OTHERS

Be kind to others unconditionally. The more you help others to feel valued, the better you will feel about yourself. Treat people with consideration and respect and be helpful in any way you can. Being of service allows you to see the way others live, from another perspective, and you could end up learning that you are more fortunate than many.

Whenever you offer help, it is important to not regard the person as a victim and to not have a covert motive such as ego gratification. So although we are focusing on self-esteem, your fulfilment must be derived only from the privilege of being able to give.

INVEST IN YOUR PERSONAL AND SPIRITUAL GROWTH

Find self-help books and positive groups to nurture your personal and spiritual growth, if this is important to you. Personal growth is a process of change that comes through self-examination and awareness and focuses on improving one's inner strength and potential. Spirituality is not tied to any particular religious belief or tradition. It involves finding meaning and purpose in life and a sense of being connected with the universe. It is deeply personal and may involve meditation, prayer and the use of chants and mantras. These are good approaches that benefit emotional health.

INTERACT SOCIALLY AND TRY NEW HOBBIES

After withdrawal ends or as you gradually improve, it is important to engage with others and to interact socially. Look for community and interest groups that offer activities in which you might be interested. Sign up for a night class to learn a new language, play an instrument, paint, write short stories or something which you have always been keen to learn. Start with a course which isn't too challenging so that it is achievable. Your success will help to build your confidence. Get a new, affordable pet. Take your dog for walks in the park and chat with other pet owners. You never know who you might meet.

RETURN TO WORK OR VOLUNTEER

If you had to give up work during withdrawal, re-employment can be a positive experience which will be beneficial in many ways. It will improve your financial situation, give you an opportunity to build new friendships, help to rebuild your confidence, give you a sense of purpose and make you feel as if you are contributing to society in some way.

Volunteering can be a good, gentle way of getting back into working life if the idea of full- or part-time work is at first too daunting. It is also a good way of getting experience that could make you more employable. You will meet new people and possibly make new friends. In addition, helping organizations and people in need will enhance your self-esteem. If the prospect of volunteering makes you feel tentative, you could try micro-volunteering. This involves doing small, manageable tasks usually via the Internet. It could be as simple as doing surveys for an organization such as Amnesty International or writing to a sick child. This will increase your feeling of self-worth and could lead to your making a bigger volunteering commitment.

MAINTAIN PHYSICAL WELLNESS

Look after your body well. If you need to lose weight, instead of dieting, exercise regularly and change your eating habits so that you lose weight gradually and keep it off. Eat fibre-rich foods including generous portions of fruit and vegetables, drink adequate amounts of water, consume complex rather than simple carbohydrates and avoid high-glycaemic foods; reduce salt and sugar intake, eat foods that contain omega-3 fatty acids and use your vitamins and supplements as a boost, and not as a substitute for nutrient-rich foods.

Ensure you get sufficient rest and sleep. For a while after recovery, limit your caffeine and alcohol intake. If you had a very difficult, intense withdrawal, be patient. Wait for at least 6 months before gently reintroducing them and do so in minute quantities at first, gradually increasing the amounts if there are no adverse reactions. This may sound overly cautious, but after all you have been through, it will be easy to do.

Explore with complementary therapies. Many people find reflexology, reiki, acupuncture, homeopathy, aromatherapy, EFT and Jin Shin Jyutsu to be helpful. If you search the Internet you will also find many others which are just as effective. When using these therapies and techniques, it is important to work with qualified, experienced practitioners.

Without disregarding conventional medicine, look at nutrition and the use of natural remedies, such as garlic and aloe vera, as alternative ways of dealing with the milder health problems. Thoroughly research whatever you choose to use and bear in mind that herbs are medicinal too. Remember, knowledge is empowering and moderation is key.

Add an exercise that is grounding and mentally balancing, such as yoga, pilates or tai chi, to your regimen. Go for walks and spend time outdoors in pleasant, natural surroundings, away from the computer and television.

MANAGE STRESS

Stress occurs when demands feel greater than one's ability to cope. There will always be stressful situations in everyday life, but after withdrawal you will want to do everything you can to keep your stress levels as low as possible. All the information in this chapter plus the coping techniques shared in Chapter 8 – such as mindfulness, meditation, positive self-talk and diaphragmatic breathing – can be used to minimize stress levels. Here are some other ways to avoid and manage stress:

- Ask for help when you need it.

- Manage your time efficiently.

- Don't take yourself or life too seriously. See the humour in everyday situations.

- See problems as opportunities rather than obstacles.

- Live within your financial means and deal promptly with debt issues.

- Share love and affection with your pet.

- Tend to your garden, if you have one. Gardening is very therapeutic.

- Clear clutter and keep your home tidy.

- Pamper yourself; have regular massages or learn to do self-massages.

- Be grateful. Daily do a mental inventory of the good in your life or keep a gratitude journal.

- Express your feelings. Find someone who will listen actively and with empathy.

- Watch feel-good movies.

- Read uplifting or enlightening books.

- Listen to music.

- Play board games and do puzzles.

- Watch sport and support your favourite teams.

- Be okay with making mistakes.

- Be tolerant of others' mistakes.

- If a situation is very stressful and you can change it, then do so.

- Live in the present moment as much as you can and let go of the past.

- Have some quiet time each day to be still and do nothing.

- Learn to recognize and avoid as many stress triggers as you can.

GET PROFESSIONAL HELP

If you are overwhelmed by the prospect of moving on or you doubt your ability to cope successfully with this post-recovery stage, please seek professional help. A counsellor or psychotherapist can help you to find other solutions, explore any underlying issues and deal with any post-traumatic effects from your withdrawal experience.

There are many therapeutic approaches, including Integrative, Existential, Eye Movement Desensitization (EMDR) and Reprocessing, Transactional Analysis (TA), Gestalt, Jungian, Person-Centred, Psychodynamic and Schema Therapy, which are very effective. Cognitive Behavioural Therapy (CBT) will help you to identify the connections between your thoughts, feelings and behaviour, and to find practical skills to manage anxiety, if pre-existing anxiety returns. Research and explore, and you will find a model that best suits your needs.

Whatever choices you make, always remember that you overcame what once seemed like an insurmountable challenge. You will cope with whatever life brings you in this new chapter. See it as an opportunity to use all the new coping techniques you learned, and the knowledge and wisdom you acquired, to create a good future. All that is left for you to do now is exhale, let go, release the withdrawal chapter and enjoy this new one that is about to unfold. Life awaits your presence.

18 SUCCESS STORIES

Writing a success story involves reliving an unpleasant experience which may trigger unwanted memories and feelings. It is fully understandable, then, that after dealing with withdrawal many people don't ever want to hear the words 'antidepressant' or 'benzo' again. They simply want to make up for lost time, resume their normal lives and forget about withdrawal. This is why people who have recovered should never be pressured to share their stories, and why I am so grateful to those who have done so here.

We are also thankful to our recovered friends who have given their kind permission for us to share excerpts from their emails in lieu of them having to relive their stories. As you will see, many thought they would never survive withdrawal. But they are all now actively engaging in life – back at work, going on exciting holidays, having good times with family and friends, and enjoying sports and other hobbies. Imagine that this is what it will be like for you when your receptors heal.

I have separated the accounts into two categories. The first comprises the protracted experiences and the second covers the experiences that are considered to be in the normal time frame (less than 18 months). Before you begin, please remember that the average duration of withdrawal is 6–18 months. Keep this in mind as you read. The protracted cases shared here are some of the worst, so please don't anticipate yours being similar. Also, usually when someone says it took three or four years for full recovery, it does not mean the entire time was spent with intense and disabling symptoms. They tend to write mainly about the worst times, but many of them had periods when things were manageable, or in some cases just a few symptoms persisted. Please don't be discouraged. Keep thinking of how resilient the nervous system is.

PROTRACTED DURATION
CARLOS: RECOVERED AND 'STRONG AT THE BROKEN PLACES'

This is what Carlos kindly sent to me when I wrote asking for his account:

My name is Carlos and this is my journey to recovery. Before I start, if you were anything like me and believe that anyone that recovered from benzo withdrawal couldn't have been as ill as you and it will never happen for you, I was exactly the same. Just don't give up. Even though you often can't see or feel it, your mind and body are slowly healing, hour by hour, day by day and month by month. Mine is an example of how not to do it. That being said I hope it will reassure you that you can recover no matter how bad it seems.

My story of psychotropic drugs started in my early 20s when a psychiatrist prescribed the antipsychotic, trifluoperazine (Stelazine), which was to help with depression and anxiety symptoms. A few years later I was struggling to cope at home and at work. I saw a doctor who prescribed paroxetine (Seroxat/Paxil) for depression to replace the Stelazine along with clomethiazole (Heminevrin) to help me sleep.

Around three years later my wife and I separated and I began having anxiety symptoms again. I went to see the doctor who this time prescribed zopiclone (Imovane) to help me sleep, replacing the Heminevrin, and I was given clonazepam (Rivotril/Klonopin) for anxiety. This helped the symptoms at first although within a year I had upped the dose of clonazepam from 0.5 mg to 1.5 mg per day due to tolerance. I noticed the clonazepam helped initially but within a few hours of taking it the anxiety would become so bad, it could get to a point I found it hard to be around people.

This was the start of years of living in a kind of purgatory where I wasn't functioning and could barely look after myself. I knew the clonazepam was probably causing this yet couldn't understand why, if this was the case, the Doctor would so easily prescribe it. I asked a psychiatrist how to get off the clonazepam and he said I could just stop it, and that I would be 'edgy for a month'. I took his advice and after around a week I found myself in hospital with numbness down one side, convinced that I was having a stroke. After tests and telling the hospital doctor what had happened it was the first time I had heard the term 'This is benzo withdrawal'.

I called my GP, got another prescription and accepted that I could probably never get free from the drug. Sometime after I found the *Ashton Manual* on the Internet and proudly took a print of the tapering sheets to my doctor. My doctor agreed to prescribe diazepam (Valium) so I could taper. My equivalent dose to the clonazepam and zopiclone was 44 mg per day; my doctor gave me 35 mg per day and was keen for me to reduce the dose as quickly as possible. I had tapered from Seroxat a year before and had just got over the 'zaps' in my head and Déjà Vu symptoms. The whole thing scared me but I filled the diazepam prescription and switched from zopiclone and clonazepam to diazepam. At best the diazepam took the edge from withdrawing from the other two pills and I had to beg the doctor not to reduce the diazepam too quickly.

At the end of the taper which took just under a year, I was unable to look after myself and had to go back to my childhood home to be looked after by my mum. It felt like a horrific version of 'Groundhog Day'. All my senses were turned up to 11, on a scale of 1 to 10. I could barely eat, food felt like glass going down my throat and my stomach was painful. I was mostly confined to my old bedroom but would go downstairs to get food and drinks and would try and go outside in the garden once a day for a few minutes to get some air.

Most days I would cry and felt better when I did. In the evenings I would watch television with the headphones on until around 5:00 or 6:00a.m. Then I would go to bed. There was a cattle grid two miles away and I could hear the cars going over it. There were chickens in a farm around half a mile away and I could hear them. I would close my eyes and my pupils would still dart round and I could see flashing lights. The muscles in my legs and arms would twitch and the muscles on the side of my head would twitch to the point where I could hear a kind of rhythmic drumming. The tinnitus was so loud I thought electrical appliances were faulty in my room. If the central heating came on, the sound of the pipes expanding would make me physically jump. Then I would sleep for three hours, sometimes less, but never more.

The worst thing was the way I felt inside, frightened and alone, thinking there were six billion people in the world and not one could help me or understand me. My phone was on silent but even it lighting up and vibrating was enough to make me jump out of my skin. Half the time I was convinced my mother was going to have the Community Mental Health services come and take me away, and the other half of the time I think I *wanted* them to take me. I just couldn't see the situation getting better.

After a few months I was able to go out for a short walk with Mum, in an area where no one was around. I also started seeing a counsellor who understood withdrawal once a week. It helped having someone there to talk to. I really did need someone to draw out what I was going through and finish my sentences as I couldn't put one together by myself.

Gradually, I started spending more time back in my own home, although I found it more stressful and would almost run from my car to the front door as I didn't want to talk to anyone or be seen. I was able to go to more appointments as long as I could park close to the door, and started getting dental care which I had ignored for years.

My doctor would send me for tests – everything from Crohn's disease to thyroid function – and the results would always be negative. He was keen for me to take antidepressants again, but I refused. During my second year off, my Dad died and I was able to go to the funeral. It wasn't easy but my family were supportive of me and I got through it. (My withdrawal has brought us all closer together.)

A few months later I started volunteering with a charity and although very difficult at first, it gave me a reason to get up and people were pleased to see me. I also got a puppy and although in the beginning I almost gave him up, the gift he gave me in getting me out every day was priceless and I love him to bits today. I also started a counselling course at a nearby college and enjoyed it. I then spent some time working with another charity on their helpline.

It has now been more than three years since I became benzo free. Earlier this year I went to Belgium with friends and was walking around the city of Bruges by myself. I kept thinking, 'This is incredible! Four years ago I wasn't able to go into a shop to buy even one item.' I've also volunteered at a music festival this year where there were 55,000 people and I enjoyed being there. I am now back at college working towards completing my counselling diploma.

My life continues to improve in every way. I'm able to sleep well, I eat healthily, and I have regained the weight I lost. I enjoy people's company and being sociable again. The main thing I've learned is how to look after myself mentally and physically. And with regard to the withdrawal, it has left me with the goal of making the best of my life as I lost a lot of years sedated from the world. I really think I'm strong at the broken places, like Hemingway said, and I'm positive about the future now.

ANNIE: A LONG JOURNEY BUT MADE IT IN THE END

Annie had terrible burning sensations, obsessive thoughts and insomnia which all surfaced during her taper off clonazepam, which she took for 11 years. She did not have any early windows of clarity and the symptoms had been relentless:

I gave up on ever being able to sleep properly again. Never had more than two hours since coming off the meds three and a half years ago. I was always agitated. I had two awful thoughts that stayed with me the whole time. I felt I would have them forever. The burning was so intense all I could do sometimes was lie in the tub in cool water. It would make it bearable for a while. I cried every day. Monday, I noticed the thoughts were gone. Now the burning is gone and last night I slept for more than seven hours.

I am crying now but this time it is not because I am scared or sad. I feel like this is a rebirth. It is taking time to sink in. This is a miracle. I refused psychiatric treatment because I knew it had to be withdrawal. I was taking the medication for anxiety and they told me the anxiety came back and this is why I was having the thoughts. When my doctor said maybe I have OCD I was scared. Now my mind is quiet for the first time in years. I am in shock. This is awesome.

The burning, insomnia and thoughts never returned. Annie now uses several approaches, including EFT and breathing, to cope with her anxiety. She has just completed a college diploma and has started a new job.

MIKE AND MARY: SIMILAR SITUATIONS, DIFFERENT EXPERIENCES

Mike took diazepam for two years. His wife, Mary, took it for almost nine years. When Mary noticed that her memory and reading comprehension were being affected, they both decided to quit. Although Mary was on it for much longer, they tapered using similar schedules over the same period of time. They both took supplements during their tapers but ended up having very different recovery processes.

Mary had very few symptoms and, after four months of what she describes as mild discomfort, felt better than all her years on the drug. She was benzo-free and fully recovered. Mike, on the other hand, had the most distressing symptoms. He had pains all over his body, with the head and back pain being almost unbearable. He also experienced many of the psychological symptoms and found the depersonalization, derealization, brain fog and obsessive thoughts, in particular, very disturbing. Sadly, these symptoms remained with him for more than three years. He could not understand how his wife had healed so quickly and why his symptoms were so unrelenting.

It was not until his 32nd month off that Mike experienced his first window. His wife could not accept that the drug could have had such an effect. She eventually concluded that something else must be wrong with him. All diagnostic tests were negative and Mike resolved to accept his symptoms and allow his healing to take place. He feels that his faith, regular use of breathing exercises and positive self-talk helped him to cope.

When Mike experienced his first few months of being symptom-free he was so worried about a flare-up that he did not tell anyone. He was thrilled but tentative – always in fear of something going wrong. He'd spent such a long time feeling unwell that his recovery was at first very surreal. He admits that for a while, he did not know how to move on. It has now been 7 months since Mike's recovery and, thankfully, he has not had the return of even one symptom. Life is back to normal for him, and he and Mary are planning a cruise this summer.

JAMES: ENJOYING LIFE AGAIN AFTER 27 MONTHS

After taking clonazepam for 14 months, James began to feel unwell. He was on a low dose of 0.125 mg daily and did a quick taper off, with no supervision. He had a relatively intense acute period with distorted perception, intense pain and burning, nausea and dizziness. At 6 months off he developed gastric problems, persistent low back pains, recurring obsessive thoughts, stitch-like cramp below his ribs, loss of appetite, high anxiety, paranoid and depressive moods.

His back pain was very severe and as a result he had diagnostic tests to rule out a suspected kidney stone. He also had other diagnostic tests, which were all negative. When he consulted a psychiatrist, he was told that his symptoms could not possibly be related to withdrawal because his dose was low. James became frustrated and was convinced he was mentally ill. Based on his doctors' opinions, there was no way his problems could have been caused by the clonazepam.

After exchanging a few emails via the website, James felt reassured that what he was experiencing was indeed due to his withdrawal. He was encouraged to try breathing and other relaxation techniques and also experimented with positive self-talk. Despite this, he felt that he was barely hanging on to his sanity and at times became convinced that he must be very, very ill with some unknown disease.

James had very few windows during his first year of being benzo-free. He felt discouraged because many of his online friends, who had been on higher doses for longer, were already having periods of feeling improved. He tried a few supplements and was disappointed and discouraged when he had a most intense flare-up of symptoms. This 'wave' continued until his 16th month off, when he had finally had a good window. More setbacks followed, but by his 27th month off, he began to feel better than he had for many years. He knew then that his full recovery was imminent. It was, and James's life is back to normal. He is now engaged to be married to an old friend who proved to be 'his rock' during his withdrawal ordeal.

SEREN: END OF A LONG CHAPTER AND A NEW BEGINNING

Seren was 19 when she was first prescribed lorazepam (Ativan) for panic attacks. She quickly developed tolerance and the dosage was periodically increased until she was on 10 mg daily. After 11 years on the drug, Seren began to feel much worse than when she initially took it. She experienced cognitive and other problems and, as she said, 'was in a total mess'. Her doctor was reluctant to help her discontinue the drug and she decided to taper off without his assistance. She tapered off over a 2-month period. She was worried about missing work, was not aware of the Ashton or any other method and just wanted to be benzo-free.

Seren had a very intense withdrawal with just about every symptom conceivable. She refers to it as 'true benzo hell'. When she wrote to me she was very frustrated and quite depressed at what she felt was slow progress. She was still experiencing terrible brain fog, muscle pain with burning, insomnia, high anxiety, mood swings and a host of other problems. She felt that her worst symptom was the terrible feeling of impending doom.

Most of her family and friends were no longer interested in her 'drama', which they felt was self-inflicted. Seren said that on many occasions she felt like giving up and was worried that she would sink into a deep depression or give in to the repetitive, suicidal thoughts she was having at the time.

Thankfully, in early 2008 she stumbled upon our old website and, for the first time in years, began to feel encouraged. She started doing the diaphragmatic breathing technique and kept talking to herself positively. She wasn't keen on affirmations but found that positively talking herself through the symptoms helped and gave her the will to survive.

A few months later, Seren experienced her first window of clarity. She was overjoyed but also quite tentative and still unsure of her recovery. It was a brief window and another wave soon came crashing. This setback threw her off course; she said it almost broke her completely.

It was also at that time that Seren became more determined than ever to make it to recovery. She felt that letting go of the process was important and made the decision to accept what was taking place. That way, she would be allowing her recovery to unfold in its own time. She started to observe her symptoms without becoming upset. Though they persisted for a few more months, this new attitude made the experience a lot less unpleasant than it had previously been.

By late 2008 Seren's symptoms started disappearing, but she waited until she was four months symptom-free before celebrating her recovery. Seren lost a lot of her prime years to Ativan, but that chapter of her life is now over. She has moved on. She says she has had no panic episodes or any return of the pre-existing anxiety. She uses all the coping techniques she learned during withdrawal to cope with her underlying condition and has no intentions of ever again taking medication for anxiety.

NORMAL DURATION
JULIAN: RECOVERED 5 MONTHS AFTER COMING OFF LORAZEPAM

Julian was prescribed 1 mg of lorazepam (Ativan) to be taken twice daily for anxiety. He took the drug for 1 year. Julian said:

I decided to taper off because I forgot to pack my medication when going on a vacation and was sick beyond belief. As soon as I returned home I took a dose and felt better. I knew then that something was wrong. So I started doing research on the web and was surprised to find all the information about withdrawal from benzodiazepines.

I decided to start my taper. First I used a pill cutter but that was just too hard for me, so I bought a jeweller's scale and one that weighs down to 0.0001 thousands. I then reduced the drug by 10 per cent of the dosage every month. I used sandpaper and a nail file to do this. It is not an exact science but it worked for me. Very slowly is the only way to go.

My withdrawal symptoms were intense but tolerable. I would say around the fifth month off is when I really started to feel like the worst was behind me. There were many times I almost gave in but I'm glad I stuck it out.

NOAH: LIFE IS CALM AFTER RECOVERY

Noah was prescribed 0.125 mg of clonazepam (Rivotril/ Klonopin) for 4–5 months for chronic pain. After having tolerance symptoms for 2 months his doctor advised him to stop taking the drug (cold turkey). His tolerance withdrawal symptoms included gnawing abdominal cramps on his right side, and when that would subside he said he would then have a stitch-like cramp slightly below his right rib which would then change into lower back soreness and pain.

He did as his doctor suggested and completely stopped taking the clonazepam. The tolerance symptoms persisted but were accompanied by high anxiety, loss of appetite, depression, panic attacks/night sweats and insomnia. This lasted for approximately 5 months.

When asked how things are now, Noah said, 'Life is calm now. Reading many of the forums helped me get through it as did keeping a log of symptoms and duration. It was a relief when I started to experience "windows of normality" and was able to see the windows gradually begin to widen.'

Noah is relieved to be over it but still feels somewhat frustrated that the established medical profession mostly fails to recognize or give any credence to 'protracted withdrawal'. His message to others going through withdrawal is, 'Don't give up hope. You will get through it.'

DIANA: RECOVERED AFTER 12 YEARS ON CLONAZEPAM AND PAROXETINE

Diana was prescribed clonazepam (Klonopin/Rivotril) and paroxetine (Paxil) after suffering a series of panic attacks and being diagnosed with panic disorder by an Emergency Room doctor. She took both drugs for 12 years. In 2010 she briefly stopped both but soon reinstated. After becoming suicidal on the paroxetine she was switched to citalopram (Celexa) and then tapered off both the citalopram and clonazepam over a 12-month period, completing her taper in March 2012.

Diana says:

> I went very slow and tried to walk as much as I could. I dealt mostly with the bad anxiety, insomnia, derealization, depersonalization, vision problems, nightmares and a lot of suicidal ideation. I had no pain or burning or tingling. At times I would forget where I was and I would look for things and not be able to read labels. I did a lot of deep breathing and spent hours on the phone speaking with positive people who were also going through withdrawal.

She played games on her iPhone, did the 4-7-8 breathing technique, affirmations, took baths, wrote in her journal, prayed, volunteered and watched 'The Big Bang Theory'.

When asked how she feels now, Diana replied:

> Looking back I have no idea how I did it. I was on for a number of years and really didn't have a clue of how blunted I really was. When I reduced to about 0.18 mg of klonopin I started to feel euphoric and excitement started to come back. Then I noticed my memory improving and that my mind was becoming clearer. I would have to say that I feel a whole lot

stronger and much happier to be alive. I thought I was never going to get better. I feel like I have a brand new life now. I don't take anything for granted anymore.

DAN'S UPDATES: RECOVERED AFTER 14 YEARS OF ANTIDEPRESSANT USE

These updates are from Dan:

For the past three months I've experienced terrible feelings of my head closing in on me. I have not been able to sleep. I feel like I'm way down inside my body and totally cut off from the world. Everything sounds like I am listening through cotton balls. The tight band feeling around my head has moved to the centre of my forehead and the nausea is severe. My whole body is burning and sizzling like I am constantly being electrocuted.

...I am really getting sick and tired of this. I feel like I want to grab it all and throw it through a window. I know you would say I need to accept and make peace with what is happening and most times I do. Today I don't have the patience. I am scared that I will not make it. Thanks for listening.

...I feel worse today. I didn't think this was possible but the agitation is terrible and my body is pounding and pulsing. Add that to the other symptoms. I do have the feeling that exercise is somehow creating central nervous system fatigue but I don't want to give it up. I guess I will have to. I can't imagine not exercising. What am I going to do? This sucks.

...Does anyone have it this bad? It's been five weeks since I have been in bed. There must be something else wrong with me. I don't believe this is still withdrawal. I am going to see my doctor. I can't go on anymore.

...I still get some of the symptoms on and off but the worst ones went away. I can't believe it. I know you told me every day that I will get better but it went on for so long, I stopped believing it was possible to get better.

...It's been four months without any symptoms. I decided to not bring my expectations to the table regarding recovery and would tell myself don't be surprised if they came back. I don't think they will. I can feel that I am healed. I am in shock but better – much better.

JEAN: FULLY RECOVERED AFTER 11 MONTHS

Jean went to her doctor complaining of indigestion and gastric reflux. He did all sorts of tests but couldn't find anything wrong. He said her problems were due to anxiety and prescribed an anti-anxiety benzo, lorazepam (Ativan). It seemed to help in the beginning but then she began to feel ill all the time. He told her to stay on it and increased the dose. She continued to feel unwell and started having panic attacks, couldn't sleep properly and had other side effects.

It wasn't until six years later that she found the information on our website and contacted us. She got her doctor to taper her off using diazepam, spending six weeks at each stage of reduction. She had problems – the classic symptoms that tend to appear – some scary and some not. Jean said she would feel her adrenaline rush, would pace up and down and had a lot of burning and nerve pain. Her hearing, vision, taste and smell were distorted and her memory was affected. For the first ten months she had no windows.

She wrote to *Recovery Road* daily and said that although she had never meditated, she gradually started breathing exercises and would listen to meditation CDs, Buddhist chants, etc. Because of her agitation she would pace up and down while listening but they still helped. She said sometimes a line from one of the chants or meditations would 'stick in her head' and replace her repetitive thoughts. It was powerful and helped her to cope better.

She also started telling herself she was getting better and that she was healing. Even when she felt very unwell and didn't believe it, she would speak positively to herself. She printed off our emails and read them over and over.

At the beginning of the 11th month she noticed the symptoms going one by one. Within 2 weeks most of them were gone. They never returned. Jean wants to share that it is possible to get better quickly, but even if it is taking longer we all get there in the end. If she could give one bit of advice it would be to try a breathing exercise. It helped to calm her. Jean says, 'Withdrawal is scary but in the end we kick it; we survive and we win'.

PAT'S UPDATES: ANTIDEPRESSANT AND BENZO RECOVERY

These updates are from Pat:

I can't eat or fall asleep. I would welcome ten minutes of sleep. I can deal with the gastrointestinal pains, the reflux, numbness and other yucky stuff but this is killing me. I don't know what to do. I don't have anything I can fall back [on]. I need sleep relief.

…I have great news! I was able to sleep last night. Thank the good Lord. I had three hours. I was a happy person before this drug took over my life. I used to sleep well all the time until Dad died. Then they gave me these drugs. The last five years have been hell. I wouldn't want this to happen to my worst enemy.

…Lately I am getting a lot of 'windows'. This is weird. One minute I feel I am going to die and in three weeks all the symptoms are going for hours at a time. I was worried that I would have to go on something to be able to sleep. I figured that's just the way it has to be. Your website kept me going and made me wait. I am happy I did.

…I am sleeping well, all through the night now. All the other symptoms have disappeared too. Just mild numbness remains and tingling some of the times. They don't bother me. I reckon this is it for me. The nightmare is over!

STEVEN: VERY FEW SYMPTOMS AND NO WITHDRAWAL

Steven said he found our website by accident and felt motivated to write to say he didn't believe so many people could be experiencing problems coming off benzos and that he didn't think there was anything called benzo withdrawal. When I replied asking about his experience he wrote again with his story, which he has kindly given us permission to share.

He was prescribed diazepam for 27 years and decided to come off because he felt it wasn't making any difference and he didn't want to be on the drug for the rest of his life. He reduced over what we would consider to be too short a period (withheld as unsafe to share) and said that other than a mild headache and slight dizziness, he had no problems. He is not on any other medication and did not use any supplements.

Although we would not recommend coming off the way he did, I hope it will encourage those yet to taper. It is true that not everyone has a nightmare withdrawal. I am sure there are many others like Steven who aren't even aware that withdrawal exists.

WILLIAM: OFF HIS BENZO AND
ANTIDEPRESSANT AND DOING WELL

William was prescribed a low dose of lorazepam over a period of three and a half months to deal with anxiety which resulted from a traumatic event. He was also taking the antidepressant, venlafaxine. Although he felt he was on the drug for a short time, he very sensibly opted to taper off by making very small cuts and holding for five weeks at each stage. During his taper he started experiencing stomach pains, restless legs, intense feelings of exhaustion, brain fog, muscle and joint pains, severe depression, insomnia, severe headaches and skin pain, which made him feel permanently sunburned.

He eventually made it to being benzo-free and, at three months off, started having mood swings with feelings of rage. His antidepressant was no longer effective and, although he continued taking it, his depression worsened. There was no light at the end of the tunnel for William. He was scared. The nightmare stories that he found on the Internet combined with having this problematic withdrawal made him feel like giving up. He even considered reinstating the benzo but decided against it.

One morning, William woke up feeling as if he was healing. This was his first window. He went on to have what he called 'good days and bad days'. Eventually his health improved enough for him to be able to return to work. At seven months off lorazepam, William felt fully recovered and was able to focus on tapering off the antidepressant. He felt that having survived benzo withdrawal, he was more than equipped to deal with quitting the antidepressant.

A year later, William was off all medication. He says that he no longer takes his health for granted and eats healthily, exercises regularly and practises meditation and yoga for relaxation. He has just completed counselling to work on the issue for which he was first prescribed the medication, and now feels optimistic and in control of his life again.

SUE'S UPDATES: QUICKLY DEPENDENT, NOW RECOVERED

These updates are from Sue:

> This cannot be happening. I was only on the benzo and antidepressant for 5 weeks. I am freaking out. My shoulder blades, upper arms and legs are burning like hell. I notice if I try to swim or go to the gym they get worse. I don't know what to do because that's the only way I can release my anger and anxiety. The pain burns too and the spasms are bad. Yesterday they went across my chest. It made me feel like I was having a heart attack. I am scared. Please help me.

...I have been hyperventilating a lot. Hubby said to get a bag and carry it around with me. It is very hard to believe I could be having this reaction after taking the medication for such a short time. This is very unfair. I didn't even have anxiety. It is hard to believe this is withdrawal. I just don't think it will go. Need some reassurance please.

...Sorry I haven't been in touch. Things got very bad for me and I wasn't coming on the Internet. This morning I thought I'd better let you know I am alive. Everything stopped and I feel like old me again. This is the craziest thing I have ever seen in my life. Amazing how it all goes away like nothing ever happened. Never again! Thanks for your help.

ALEX'S UPDATES: LORAZEPAM AND PAROXETINE RECOVERY

These updates are from Alex:

I don't know what to do. I keep feeling worse and worse. I just can't eat or drink, [...] agitated, feelings of rage, nausea, muscle pain and burning, head tremors, body tremors, and feel like my brain is dead. I can't walk. I'm very weak and can't bathe myself. It seems like it's more than withdrawal, but I don't know what it could be. All the lab tests at the hospital were normal. This is cruel. The suffering is so great.

...Old childhood traumas are coming back. The depersonalization and derealization make me feel totally disconnected. I have tantrums all the time and can't think like an adult or say anything that makes sense. It's like I am a child again.

...Thank you for writing all of this. I have gotten to the point where I just don't want to live, anymore. I feel out of touch with the real world like a psychotic person. I have never felt like this before. I feel I want to die. I feel helpless. Is this ever going to end?

…What if I am in denial? I feel so messed up in my head, I can't describe it. I am tired. I am drained. Tired of fighting. I'm tired of trying to explain to my family, my friends, my doctors. Why doesn't anyone understand? I am normally a very together person. Now I feel helpless and desperate. Please write soon. Your emails are helping me a lot.

…I'm feeling so good these days, weeks pass with no thoughts about withdrawal. I feel almost 100 per cent healed. I still have the odd day where I feel a bit like symptoms are hanging on but hardly. It's as if my brain decided it had enough. Who says we don't get better? We do! Hope you are doing fine.

MICHELLE: RECOVERED AND HEALTHY AFTER DETOX

Michelle took lorazepam (Ativan) for 12 years. She was taken off over three weeks in a detox centre. All seemed to be well until she started having very intense reactions with every conceivable symptom surfacing after she was discharged. When she contacted us she was having seizure-type movements. We advised her to see her doctor immediately to be reinstated. Her doctor did so, then gradually tapered her off substituting with diazepam, reducing her dosage every four weeks and sometimes every five or six weeks.

She was very fortunate in that she had a very successful taper with quite mild symptoms. After completing her taper she continued to feel better and within 1 year of being benzo-free felt that she was fully recovered. Thankfully, she was reinstated in time and avoided a protracted, problematic recovery process. (Please note that detox over such short periods is very dangerous and should be avoided, even when anti-seizure medication is given. The problems usually begin after discharge. We receive calls of this nature daily.)

LIAM: WELL AGAIN AFTER VALIUM AND PROZAC

Liam was prescribed diazepam and was later given fluoxetine after his father died. He tapered off diazepam after being in tolerance withdrawal for more than a decade. At the time he didn't know about tolerance and thought other medical problems were causing him to be unwell. He tapered off reducing by 10 per cent of his dose every four weeks. He was able to withdraw successfully with just the tolerance symptoms he was already experiencing, plus a few others which he described as being not very intense.

Six months later he decided to come off the fluoxetine. After he completed his taper off this antidepressant he said he felt worse than after his diazepam taper, but the symptoms were still manageable. When he contacted us his main concern was having inappropriate sexual thoughts and feelings. He noticed that when he had them he also had burning, nausea and agitation. He said they felt 'chemical' and would appear out of the blue.

Once he discovered that having these unwanted thoughts was a common symptom, he accepted they had nothing to do with his rational mind and did not give them any attention or struggle against them. The thoughts, along with the burning and other symptoms, disappeared before his second-year anniversary of being drug-free.

Liam said he was initially scared but decided to not struggle against whatever transpired. He was determined to succeed at becoming benzo-free. He is now fully recovered and is enjoying a quality of life he never imagined he could have.

NICKY'S UPDATES: RECOVERED FROM ANTIDEPRESSANT WITHDRAWAL

These updates are from Nicky:

This taper is scary. I feel desperate. My family and friends keep telling me I need to go back to the doctor to get something to help. I think they feel I have another problem. I don't like writing my symptoms because it frightens me to death. I just can't see how I am going to get better. I know you say I must keep telling myself I will. But I don't believe it. Sorry.

...The fear is with me 24/7. I am always agitated to the point of akathisia. It never goes away. Some days I tell myself I just need to accept it and other days I just cry all day. I am scared and sad all the time. I can cope with the other symptoms but this is unbearable. I want to wake up and feel normal. Will that day ever come?

...It's so bad these days – so many symptoms. My bladder is messed up and I can hardly detect when I have to pee. I am having tremors with the agitation this morning, very nauseous, highly anxious. I don't know how I am meant to go on like this.

...I'm so afraid. I feel disconnected, like a zombie. I can barely walk or stand up. The good news is that the agitation is getting better now and I have times when my body is quiet. If this dreamlike state would go I think I would feel okay, like I can cope. Everyone says not to stress but it's hard to go through this and not feel like you're about to die.

...Finally, I am having better days. The agitation is completely gone and I am beginning to feel connected again. I still feel heavy and like I have constant flu but compared to a few months ago this isn't bad. As you've said again and again, this too shall pass. I think it is passing. I am trying not to get too happy yet in case it all comes back.

...I thought you would enjoy hearing about the positive news because you have been patient with me for so long. I don't have symptoms anymore. They don't seem to be planning on coming back. This has been the hardest thing I have ever had to do in my life and I have been around a long time. I never thought this insanity would end but it has.

Happy endings are always encouraging. The most difficult stories to obtain are from the people who had no problems or just very few, mild symptoms. As previously mentioned, most of them do not frequent the Internet support groups and some are not aware that withdrawal even exists. However, all you really need to know is that there are numerous success stories and we do recover from withdrawal. Like the many thousands before you, including me and these survivors who have shared here, you will overcome this overwhelming experience. Expect your nervous system to heal and trust that you, too, will one day celebrate your recovery.

RESOURCES

WITHDRAWAL SUPPORT PROJECTS AND HELPLINES

Battle Against Tranquillisers
National Helpline Tel: 0117 966 3629 or 0844 826 9317
Website: www.bataid.org

Bristol and District Tranquilliser Project
National Helpline Tel: 0117 962 8874
Website: www.btpinfo.org.uk

Council Against Involuntary Tranquilliser Addiction (CITA)
National Helpline Tel: 0151 932 0102
Website: www.citawithdrawal.org.uk

MIND in Camden Minor Tranquilliser Service
Helpline Tel: 020 7911 0816
Website: www.mindincamden.org.uk/mtproject.htm

Oldham Tranx Support Group
Tel: 0145 787 6355 – Barry Haslam

INFORMATION WEBSITES

Antidepressants and benzodiazepines: www.recovery-road.org
Antidepressants: www.paxilprogress.org
Comprehensive information: www.benzo.org.uk

EMOTIONAL FREEDOM TECHNIQUE (EFT)

Paula Kovacs, qualified EFT practitioner and benzo survivor

Website: www.benzorecovery.co.uk

SUICIDE HELPLINES

Samaritans (UK)

Tel: 08457 90 90 90

Website: www.samaritans.org

Samaritans (Republic of Ireland)

Tel: 1850 60 90 90

Website: www.samaritans.org

National Suicide Prevention Lifeline (USA)

Tel: 1-800-273-TALK or 1-800-273-8255

Website: www.suicidepreventionlifeline.org

Worldwide helpline numbers: www.befrienders.org

COMMON ANTIDEPRESSANTS

Generic Name	Brand Name	Type
Amitriptyline	Elavil, Tryptizol, Tryptomer	Tricyclic
Citalopram	Cipramil, Celexa	SSRI
Clomipramine	Anafranil	Tricyclic
Dosulepin	Prothiaden, Dothep	Tricyclic
Doxepin	Sinequan, Adapine, Doxal	Tricyclic
Duloxetine	Cymbalta, Ariclaim	SNRI
Fluoxetine	Prozac, Sarafem, Fontex	SSRI
Imipramine	Tofranil	Tricyclic
Lofepramine	Gamanil, Tymelyt, Lomont	Tricyclic
Mirtazapine	Remeron, Avanza, Zispin	NaSSA
Nortriptyline	Allegron, Sensoval, Aventyl	Tricyclic
Paroxetine	Seroxat, Paxil, Aropax	SSRI
Reboxetine	Edronax, Norebox, Prolift	NRI
Sertraline	Zoloft, Lustral	SSRI
Trazodone	Molipaxin, Deprax, Desyrel	SARI
Venlafaxine	Effexor	SNRI

SSRI = selective serotonin re-uptake inhibitor; SNRI = serotonin and noradrenaline re-uptake inhibitor; NaSSA = noradrenaline-specific serotoninergic antidepressant; NRI = noradrenaline re-uptake inhibitor; SARI = serotonin antagonist and re-uptake inhibitor

COMMON BENZODIAZEPINES

Generic Name	Brand Name
Alprazolam	Xanax
Bromazepam	Lexotan, Lexomil
Chlordiazepoxide	Librium
Clobazam	Frisium
Clonazepam	Klonopin, Rivotril
Clorazepate	Tranxene
Diazepam	Valium, Ducene
Flunitrazepam	Rohypnol
Flurazepam	Dalmane
Lorazepam	Ativan
Nitrazepam	Mogadon
Nordazepam	Nordaz, Calmday
Oxazepam	Serax, Serepax, Serenid
Temazepam	Restoril, Normison
Triazolam	Halcion

BENZODIAZEPINE EQUIVALENCE TABLE

Benzodiazepine	Half-Life (hrs) [active metabolite]	Approximate Equivalent Oral Dosages (mg)
Alprazolam (Xanax)	6–12	0.5
Bromazepam (Lexotan, Lexomil)	10–20	5–6
Chlordiazepoxide (Librium)	5–30 [36–200]	25
Clobazam (Frisium)	12–60	20
Clonazepam (Klonopin, Rivotril)	18–50	0.5
Clorazepate (Tranxene)	[36–200]	15
Diazepam (Valium)	20–100 [36–200]	10
Flunitrazepam (Rohypnol)	18–26	1
Flurazepam (Dalmane)	[40–250]	15–30
Lorazepam (Ativan)	10–20	1
Nitrazepam (Mogadon)	15–38	10
Nordazepam (Nordaz, Calmday)	36–200	10
Oxazepam (Serax, Serepax, Serenid)	4–15	20
Temazepam (Restoril, Normison, Euhypnos)	8–22	20
Triazolam (Halcion)	2	0.5

Z-DRUGS

Generic Name	Brand Name
Zaleplon	Sonata
Zolpidem	Ambien, Stilnoct
Zopiclone	Zimovane, Imovane
Eszopiclone	Lunesta

Note: These drugs have effects similar to those of benzodiazepines.

Z-DRUG EQUIVALENCE TABLE

Z-drug	Half-Life (hrs)	Approximate Equivalent Oral Dosages (mg)
Zaleplon (Sonata)	2	20
Zolpidem (Ambien, Stilnoct)	2	20
Zopiclone (Zimovane, Imovane)	5–6	15
Eszopiclone (Lunesta)	6 (9 in elderly)	3

Note: The two equivalence tables for Benzodiazepine and Z-drugs are useful for understanding the dosage and half-life of each drug. For example, 0.5 mg of clonazepam is equivalent to approximately 10 mg of diazepam, so someone taking 1.5 mg of clonazepam is taking the equivalent of 30 mg of diazepam, and it would take between 18 and 50 hours for half of the drug to be eliminated or for the blood concentration level to fall by half.

SYMPTOMS A TO Z

The list below includes verbatim descriptions and is intended to be used as a reference only. The withdrawal experience is unique and you may end up *not* having any of these symptoms. If you do, they may be mild and last for a very short period. This cannot be stressed enough. If you have already started tapering and are experiencing symptoms, please refer to only those that apply. It is advisable to *not* read this prior to tapering.

A

Abdominal cramps: cramping and pain in the abdomen, sometimes moving to different areas

Achiness: dull aches and pains all over the body

Agitation: restless, feeling a need to move around, 'antsy' feeling, akathisia

Agoraphobia: fear of going out, fear of open spaces, fear of having panic attacks in unfamiliar places, often confined to home

Akathisia: severe agitation, inability to sit still, feel as if wanting to climb the walls

Anger/rage: often unexplained tantrums, loss of temper with no apparent cause, feeling of wanting to 'explode'

Anxiety: adrenaline rushes, panic attacks, over-breathing, palpitations often including agoraphobia

Apathy: lack of motivation, lack of interest in self or others, emotionally flat, socially withdrawn, flatness

Appetite changes: loss, gain leading to increase or decrease in weight

B

Back pain: lower, mid, upper, coccyx

Balance problems/dizziness: feeling unsteady on feet, room 'spinning' even when sitting or lying, feeling drunk

Benzo belly: distension, bloat, pot belly, abnormally large, looking 'pregnant'

Bloating/water retention: oedema, swollen feet, swollen hands, eyelids, looking puffy

Blurred vision: everything appears blurred, problems reading and seeing generally

Body temperature: fluctuations, elevated temperature, chills

Brain fog: feeling as if observing through a cloud, reduced clarity

Brain motion: feeling of the brain moving inside head

Bruxism/teeth grinding: occurs during sleep (often associated with tolerance or as a side effect while still on drug)

Burning pain/sensations: on any part of body, often the shoulders, back, hands and feet

C

Concentration loss: inability to focus attention and/or acquire new information

Confusion: simple tasks are difficult, unable to decipher directions or follow simple instructions

Crawling sensation on skin: formication – feeling as if insects are crawling on or under skin (usually during acute withdrawal)

Creaking joints: creaking with movement, 'cracking' sound in neck, arms, back, hips

Crying spells: feeling weepy at times without being able to identify a specific trigger, inability to stop crying

D

Depersonalization: altered perception, dissociated feelings, detached from self, feeling like alien in own body, disconnected

Depressive mood: low, heavy mood, flat affect, unmotivated, feeling of hopelessness

Derealization: altered perception, dissociated feelings, feeling of being distant, cut off, being in a dream-like state, surreal

Dizziness/balance problems: unsteady on feet, feeling as if drunk, room 'spinning' even when sitting or lying

Dreams: vivid, recurring, themed, nightmares with disturbing images

Dry mouth: mouth dry and feeling as if no saliva

E

Electric shock sensations/zaps: feeling as if shocked, shocks running through body (any part including ears)

Emotional blunting or anaesthesia: inability to feel emotions whether positive or negative, not connected to authentic feelings

Exhaustion: extreme weakness, feeling totally without energy as if just completed a marathon, 'bone tired'

Extreme thirst: insatiable urge to keep drinking

Eyes: sore, dry, red/bloodshot, tired, blurred vision, double vision, swollen, floaters, glazed, glassy appearance

F

Face pain: face hurts all the time

Facial numbness: face numb, forehead numb, no feeling in one side of face, no feeling in both sides of face

Facial tingling: face tingles and has pins-and-needles sensation

False sensations of moving (perception distortion): feel as if body is moving or chair or bed

Fatigue/lethargy: extreme tiredness, listlessness, lacking in energy

Fear (organic)/impending doom: fear surpassing natural anxiety or concerns regarding withdrawal, not identifiable with a thought or feeling, feels inauthentic but overwhelming, scared that something 'terrible' is about to happen, intense fear of dying

Fits: epileptic-like movements (rare, usually as a result of cold turkey or detox)

Flu-like symptoms: feel as if getting flu with aches, joint/muscle pain, feverish, stuffy nose

G

Gastrointestinal disturbances/stomach problems: vomiting, nausea, diarrhoea, constipation, reflux, oesophageal spasms, feeling of choking, distension, stomach cramps

Glassy eyes: eyes look like those of a street drug addict's, glazed and shiny

H

Hair: change in texture, hair loss, breakage

Hallucinations: hypnagogic hallucinations or brief events when falling asleep, usually visual, tactile, sensual or auditory

Headaches/tight band around head: feeling as if an imaginary band around head is constantly being tightened, throbbing pain in head, migraine-like headaches, pain in temples

Hearing hypersensitivity/hyperacusis: exaggerated sound, cutlery, crockery, environmental sounds 'nerve-shatteringly loud', people sound as if they are shouting

Heart: palpitations, irregular beats, thumping, beating loudly, feels as if jumping out of chest cavity

Heaviness: part of the body, especially limbs, feel extremely heavy, body feels like 'lead'

Hormonal imbalances: including non-menopausal hot flashes, severe pre-menstrual tension

I

Inner trembling/shaking/vibrating (perception distortion): feeling of body trembling or vibrating 'on the inside'

Insomnia/sleep disturbances: nights at a time without sleep, few hours of sleep per night, waking up throughout the night, unable to go back to sleep

Intrusive memories: unwanted and persistent memory sometimes of traumatic events

Irritability: very low tolerance levels, easily irritated

J

Jelly legs: legs feel weak and rubbery as if about to give way

Joint/muscle pain: joints hurt, joints feel arthritic and muscles hurt, muscles feel as if have performed rigorous exercise

Jumpiness: on edge, startled by sounds or people, extremely nervous

L

Lethargy/fatigue: extreme tiredness, listlessness, lacking in energy, unable to even sit up

Libido loss: loss of interest in sexual intercourse, inability to become aroused

Light hypersensitivity: everything seems intensely and unbearably bright, feeling the need to wear sunglasses even inside, unable to look at computer screen

M

Memory impairment: short-term memory loss, 'gaps' in memory where unable to recall specific events, memory lapses (side effect of drug as well as symptom)

Menstrual irregularity and dysmenorrhoea: cycle changes and becomes irregular, painful periods

Metallic tastes: mouth has a metallic taste, gustatory distortion

Mood swings: extreme and rapid changes in moods, one minute feeling optimistic then very low, feeling 'bipolar', feeling manic then depressed

Moving sensations: false perceptions of body moving

Muscle/joint pain: joints feel arthritic and muscles stiff and hurting, muscles feel as if have performed rigorous exercise

Muscle twitches/jerks/spasms: involuntary movements – myoclonic jerks, tics, twitches and spasms in different areas of body including extremities

Muscular rigidity: muscles all over feel extremely stiff, inability to move agilely

N

Nail discolouration and splitting: nails change colour, nails yellow, look jaundiced, nails grey, weak and splitting

Nausea: feeling of wanting to throw up all the time, feeling of being seasick

Nightmares: vivid, unpleasant, sometimes terrifying dreams

Numbness/tingling: like paraesthesia, fingers, hand, face, sometimes entire body

O

Obsessive thoughts: repetitive, unwanted thoughts – often morbid thoughts about illness, death, suicide ideation and taboo sexual subjects

Oedema/water retention: fluid in body tissues, swollen feet, puffiness

Oesophageal problems: oesophageal spasms, reflux

Over-breathing: breathing faster and deeper than necessary, hyperventilating

P

Pain: different parts or all of body stiff and hurting, 'travelling' pain

Palpitations: heart races, beats wildly, thumps, feels like jumping out of chest

Panic attacks: adrenaline rushes, feel as if dying, feeling unable to breathe, feel as if choking

Paranoid thoughts: unfounded, suspicious thoughts, feel threatened, feel persecuted

Perception distortion:

a. Speech is distorted, unable to follow a conversation, time delay or inability to reconcile words being uttered with movement of mouth

b. False sensations of moving, e.g. feeling as though falling through bed, chair or as if part of body is moving away

c. Visual (seeing 'things'), e.g. flashing lights, inanimate objects appear to be moving, people appear flat, one-dimensional and paper-like, buildings leaning, undulating floors (wave-like movement)

d. Gustatory distortion, metallic taste in mouth

e. Tactile distortion, feeling of insects crawling on or under the skin (formication)

Period-related issues: intensification of symptoms at time of monthly period, severe period pain, amenorrhoea (absence of period)

Pins and needles: sensation of tingling, pricking or numbness

Profuse sweating/perspiring: rivulets of perspiration, bathed in perspiration but not feeling hot, sweating all the time even in air conditioning, often during acute withdrawal

R

Rage/anger: feeling violent, surge of anger, argumentative 'out of the blue', feeling urge to 'lash out', feeling 'about to explode'

Reading/comprehension problems: inability to read, focus or understand even simple instructions

Repetitive/obsessive thoughts: thoughts persist and interrupt cognition, can't stop unwanted thoughts going over and over in mind

Restless legs: sensation in legs, overwhelming urge to move legs when lying down, leg jerks while sleeping

S

Sexual dysfunction: loss of libido, erectile dysfunction, loss of interest in sexual intercourse

Sexually inappropriate thoughts: thoughts of taboo sexual content which are out of character and surfaced during withdrawal

Shaking/tremors: uncontrollable shaking and tremors, hands shake, part of body or whole body trembles

Skin problems: rashes, acne, itching, burning, stripping, peeling and other problems on different areas of skin

Sleep disturbance/insomnia: nights at a time without sleep, few hours of sleep per night, waking up throughout the night, unable to go back to sleep, sleeping during the day but not at night

Soft tissue pain: thighs and other fleshy areas of body hurt

Stomach problems/gastrointestinal problems: vomiting, diarrhoea, nausea, reflux, oesophageal spasms, feeling of choking, distension, stomach cramps

Sweating: profuse sweating regardless of temperature, body washed in perspiration, clothes wet

Sweats/chills: one minute perspiring profusely then freezing/shaking, hot flashes as if menopausal then shaking, hot then chills, as if one has ague

T

Temperature: fluctuations in body temperature

Thoughts: repetitive, unwanted, obsessive, suicidal

Throat: sore, tight, choking sensation, spasming

Tinnitus: constant or intermittent ringing in the ears, high-pitched noise in ears

Tiredness: exhausted, void of energy

Tooth/gum/mouth pain: nerves in teeth hurt, gum hurts, all teeth in mouth hurt

Touch hypersensitivity: extreme sensitivity to touch

Tremors/shaking: uncontrollable shaking and tremors, hands shake, part of body or whole body trembles

Twitching/tics: muscles in different areas of body twitch, involuntary movements, vocal tics

U

Uncontrollable crying: unable to stop crying (for no apparent reason)

Undulation misperception: floor and furniture appear wave-like and to be moving

Urinary problems: frequency, urinary tract infections, partial or complete incontinence, bladder hypersensitivity, dysuria

V

Vision blurred or double: everything appears blurred, problems reading, seeing 'double'

Visual perception distortion: seeing 'things', inanimate objects appear to be moving, people and objects appear flat, one-dimensional and paper-like

W

Water retention/oedema: fluid in body tissues, swollen feet, puffiness

Weakness: feel drained of energy, almost unable to move or even sit up

Weepiness: spontaneous crying spells without being able to identify a specific trigger

Weight issues: unexplained fluctuations in weight, inability to gain weight, inability to lose weight, benzo belly

Z

Zaps: electric shock sensations, feeling as if shocked, shocks running through body (any part including ears)

BIBLIOGRAPHY

Ashton, C. H. (2002) *Benzodiazepines: How They Work and How to Withdraw.* Available at www.benzo.org.uk, accessed on 26 June 2006.

Boutenko, V. (2005) *Green For Life.* Ashland, OR: Raw Family Publishing.

British National Formulary 63 (2012) London: British Medical Association & Royal Pharmaceutical Society of Great Britain.

Foster, H. (2004) *Easy G I Diet: Using the Glycaemic Index to Lose Weight and Gain Energy.* London: Octopus Publishing.

Freeman, D. and Garety, P. A. (2004) *Paranoia: The Psychology of Persecutory Delusions.* Hove: Psychology Press.

Greenblatt D. J., Shader R. I., Divoll M. and Harmatz, J. S. (1981) 'Benzodiazepines: a summary of pharmacokinetic properties.' *British Journal of Clinical Pharmacology 11*, 1, 11S–16S. Available at www.ncbi. nlm.nih.gov/pubmed/6133528, accessed on 11 January 2009.

Hay, L. L. (1999) *You Can Heal Your Life.* Carlsbad, CA: Hay House Publishing.

Jongsma, E. and Peterson, L. (2003) *Complete Adult Psychotherapy Treatment Planner.* Hoboken, NJ: John Wiley & Sons.

Lader M., Tylee A. and Donoghue J. (2009) 'Withdrawing benzodiazepines in primary care.' *CNS Drugs 23*, 1, 19–34.

Miller, W. R. and Rollnick, S. (2002) *Motivational Interviewing.* New York, NY: Guildford Press.

Rang, H. P., Dale, M. M. and Ritter, J. M. (1999) *Pharmacology* (4th ed.). Edinburgh: Churchill Livingstone.

Sommers-Flanagan, J. and Sommers-Flanagan, R. (2002) *Clinical Interviewing* (3rd ed.). Hoboken, NJ: John Wiley & Sons.

Weekes, C. (1977) *Self-Help for Your Nerves.* London: Thorsons.

Wisneski, L. A. and Anderson, L. (2004) *The Scientific Basis of Integrative Medicine.* Boca Raton, FL: CRC Press.

Woods, M. G. and Williams, D. C. (1996) 'Multiple forms and locations for the peripheral-type benzodiazepine receptor.' *Biochemical Pharmacology 52*, 12, 1805–1814.

World Health Organization (1964) 'WHO Expert Committee on Addiction-Producing Drugs.' Thirteenth report of the WHO Expert Committee (WHO Technical Report Series, No. 273). Geneva: World Health Organization.

Zeig, J. K. (1980) *A Teaching Seminar with Milton H. Erickson, M.D.* New York, NY: Brunner/Mazel.

INDEX

MANAGING STRESS WITH QIGONG

GORDON FAULKNER

Foreword by Carole Bridge

Published by Singing Dragon

Paperback: £14.99/ $24.95
ISBN: 978 1 84819 035 1
256 pages

• •

The ancient Chinese practice of Qigong combines physical movement with gentle breathing techniques to promote harmony between body and mind, and is quickly gaining popularity in the West.

This step-by-step guide to managing stress through Qigong begins by looking at stress and our response to it from both an Eastern and a Western perspective. The core of the book provides a program with first a series of carefully designed stress relief exercises, followed by a series of gentler stress prevention exercises, all of which are clearly explained with easy-to-follow instructions for each of the steps, and fully illustrated. The author explains the theory underpinning the Qigong exercises in terms of the principles of Chinese Medicine, including Yin and Yang, the Five Elements and the circulation of energy (Qi) through the meridians. Extensively trialled with Maggie's Cancer Care Centres, and designed specifically to fit around a busy lifestyle, the Qigong program set out in this book will help to reduce stress, decrease anxiety and restore energy.

This practical book will help anyone who is prone to stress, regardless of their level of ability or experience of Qigong. It will also be a useful resource for Taijiquan and Qigong instructors, alternative therapists, and other professionals working with clients who are affected by stress.

• •

Contents: Foreword. Preface. Introduction. Stress. Background to Daoyin. Practice. Basic Movements. Standing Stress Relief. Seated Stress Relief. Standing Stress Prevention. Seated Stress Prevention. Principles of Action. General Principles. Specific Principles. Appendix A: Five Elements. Appendix B: Energy System. Appendix C: Chinese Names. Glossary. Index.

✱ **Gordon Faulkner** is Prinicpal Instructor at the Chanquanshu School of Daoist Arts. He is a Certified International Judge of Daoyin Yangsheng Gong and President of the Scotland and Wales Daoyin Yangsheng Gong Association. Gordon is a closed-door student of Professor Zhang Guangde, founder of the modern Daoyin Yangsheng system taught at the Beijing Sports University.

MANAGING DEPRESSION WITH QIGONG

FRANCES GAIK

Published by Singing Dragon

Paperback: £12.99/ $19.95
ISBN: 978 1 84819 018 4
192 pages

•••

Many people will suffer from depression at some time in their lives. New research shows that Qigong, a traditional Chinese practice, can be an effective treatment for depression and can provide a good alternative or supplement to medication in some cases. Frances Gaik explains the basics of what Qigong is and why it is effective for depression, and shows the reader how to make use of Qigong to rise from the darkness of depression and regain strength and motivation in life.

Based on the same principles as Traditional Chinese Medicine, Qigong works by promoting the movement of health-giving energy along the meridians of the body. The author shows how the practical application of Qigong can radically improve health and wellbeing, and provides a treatment plan, including Qigong exercises. Encouraging the reader to identify their problems and take action, Dr. Frances Gaik gives practical advice that will help anyone with depression to improve their mental health.

Managing Depression with Qigong provides a guide to an effective and increasingly recognised form of treatment that will be invaluable to people with depression and their families.

•••

Contents: Introduction. Chapter 1. A Paradigm Shift Toward Holistic Interventions. Chapter 2. The Information System of Your Body. Chapter 3. Traditional Chinese Medicine and Qigong. 4. Identifying Your Problem. Chapter 5. Practical Applications of Qigong to Depression—The Action Plan. Chapter 6. Taking Personal Responsibility For Your Health. Chapter 7. The Clinical Research Study. Appendix. Part One: Active Exercises. Part Two: Supplementary Exercises. Part Three: Sitting Meditations. References. Acknowledgments. Index.

✳ **Frances Gaik** is a licensed clinical professional counselor, in private practice in the western suburbs of Chicago, Illinois. She holds a Doctorate in Clinical Psychology from the Adler School of Professional Psychology, and an undergraduate degree in Philosophy with a concentration on ethics. Dr. Gaik is Board Certified in Professional Counseling and is a long-term meditator and Qigong practitioner who utilizes alternative energy therapies as well as hypnosis in her therapeutic approach. She has also worked in the health insurance industry for over 25 years.

PRINCIPLES OF EFT (EMOTIONAL FREEDOM TECHNIQUES)
WHAT IS IT, HOW IT WORKS, AND WHAT IT CAN DO FOR YOU

LAWRENCE PAGETT WITH PAUL MILLWARD

Foreword by Dr Silvia Hartmann

Published by Singing Dragon

Paperback: £9.99/ $19.95
ISBN: 978 1 84819 190 7
208 pages

● ●

This is the definitive introductory guide to Emotional Freedom Techniques (EFT), a therapeutic psychological tool that draws on Chinese medicine and NLP (Neurolinguistic Programming) to remove blockages within the energy system.

Traditional and modern approaches of EFT are explained alongside a comprehensive description of EnergyEFT, the most advanced and evolved form. Simple practical usages of EFT for stress reduction are included, with step-by-step instruction on how to use tapping to remove stress and energise yourself. There are case studies and practical examples demonstrating how EFT can relieve a wide range of negative emotional conditions including anxiety, anger, depression, insomnia and migraines. The book also explores how EFT can improve and maximise positive emotional and spiritual functioning in terms of health and wealth transformation.

The uses of EFT are numerous and this handbook is an ideal starting point for anyone interested in learning more about the positive impact EFT techniques can have on their wellbeing.

● ●

Contents: Foreword by Dr Silvia Hartmann. Introduction. 1. Tracing the Ancient Origins of Asian Energy Concepts. 2. Historical Exploration of Western Applications of Eastern Energy Modalities. 3. The Birth of Tapping: Goodheart, Diamond and Callahan. 4. The Emergence of EFT: The Work of Gary Craig. 5. The Evolution of EFT: From Craig to Hartmann. 6. Tapping into the Power of EFT: DIY EFT for the Beginner. 7. Real Life Stories of EFT at Work. 8. What is Energy EFT?: The Work of Dr Silvia Hartmann. 9. Putting the Energy into EFT: The Practical Benefits of Energy Utilisation. 10. A Client's Perspective of a Professional EFT/ Energy EFT Session. Useful Organisations and Contacts. Index.

✳ **Lawrence Pagett** is a fully registered and qualified hypnotherapist with ten years' experience with a private practice. He has been tutored by Dr Silvia Hartmann to become a Master Practitioner in EnergyEFT.

✳ **Paul Millward** is a freelance writer and commentator on spiritual subjects and a proponent of EFT techniques.

PRINCIPLES OF NLP
WHAT IT IS, HOW IT WORKS, AND WHAT IT CAN DO FOR YOU

JOSEPH O'CONNOR AND IAN MCDERMOTT

Foreword by Robert Dilts

Published by Singing Dragon

Paperback: £9.99/ $15.95
ISBN: 978 1 84819 161 7
176 pages

• •

Neuro-Linguistic Programming (NLP) teaches how to model excellence to achieve excellence in everything you do. This introductory guide explains the principles of NLP and how to use these principles in your life—personally, spiritually and professionally.

By focusing on the fundamental presuppositions of NLP, this clear and concise book gets right to its core. It explains key concepts such as building rapport, modelling, anchoring and uncovering your preferred learning style. It shows how to be in tune with your patterns of behaviour and language and those of the people around you, and how to use this knowledge to reach your goals.

From building confidence, to beating depression, to career development, the uses of NLP are innumerable. This book is an ideal starting point for anyone interested in learning the life-changing techniques of NLP.

• •

Contents: Foreword by Robert Dilts. Introduction. 1. The Four Pillars of Wisdom. 2. That Is Not What I Meant at All... 3. The Ultimate Question. 4. Getting in a State. 5. Reality Leaves a Lot to the Imagination. 6. Customizing your Brain. 7. The Gatekeepers at the Doors of Perception. 8. Language, Trance and Stories. 9. Beliefs and Beyond. Resources. 1. Presuppositions of NLP. 2. Glossary. 3. Bibliography. 4. Meditation. About the Authors. Index.

✳ **Joseph O'Connor** is a leading trainer in coaching and Neuro-Linguistic Programming (NLP) and systemic thinking. He is co-founder of the International Coaching Community (ICC); co-founder and director of ROI Coaching, specialist coaching for financial executives; co-founder of the Master Coach Academy Europe; and he is Visiting Professor of Coaching, ISCTE University Business School, Lisbon, Portugal. He spent many years as a professional classical guitarist and has an L.R.A.M. from the Royal Academy of Music.

✳ **Ian McDermott** is an UKCP accredited psychotherapist. He was named one of Britain's Top 10 Coaches and is on the Association for Coaching's Global Advisory Panel. He founded International Teaching Seminars (ITS) in 1988 to provide practical skills-based training in effective change technologies for individuals and organizations in both the public and private sector. Ian was appointed External Faculty at Henley Business School and is also an Honorary Fellow of Exeter University Business School.